D0240184

£10 10

A
Welsh
Miscellany

Zymurgy Publishing, 2004

The moral right of Amanda Thomas, the author
has been asserted.

A CIP catalogue record for this book is available from the
British Library

Cover design by Nick Ridley

10 9 8 7 6 5 4 3 2 1

Printed and bound by Clowes Limited, Suffolk, U.K.

ISBN 1 903506 11 5

Published by Zymurgy Publishing, Newcastle upon Tyne
© 2004 Zymurgy Publishing

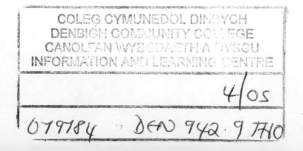

For my family and other mammals.

Thanks

The author has mostly been thinking about 'Rape of the Fair Country' and creative uses for leeks on a rainy night in Gower for the past year, but has been distracted by and gives serious thanks to:

Cath-for always ALWAYS being there. Yvonne-for continuing to entertain and inspire from the other side. Rach-for reminding me that plants have feelings too. Peter Hill-for nicking my best lines and passing them off as his own. Peter Jones-for using my best lines against me. Kevlar-for putting up with me and for being as much of an obscure-ist as I am. Marty-for believing in me and making me drink the Landlord when we have editorial meetings. Donna-for making it through the mire and not letting me wallow in it. Essops and Jonesey-for being a harbour in the tempest. Clinda-for blinding me with insolence and being my Lady Macbeth. Jane, Bern, Emily, Jack and Grandma Renee-you can now read ME like a book. Sarah-for inspiring me to put it out there. Marcus-for helping me through the difficult Kriek and Framboise years. Ceri Vale-a big 'diolch' for contributing a verse. Jez, Juz, Stan, Rhi, Lloyd of the Rings, Wes, JB and Lisa, Gits and Gwi, Fi, Kazzastan, Billfredo, Apes, Selm. Paula and Louise-for the surgical support, Hanover Square support chats, Remos sessions and for keeping me from falling out of so many windows. Ems, Christine, Kimmy, Leeroy Evans for owning up to being from Llandudno, Justin Meredith for letting his glorious roots show, Rich T, Carlsberg, Karen, Manish, B Sting, Bextor, Shazza, Andy Coker, Bunchy, Trevski, Chats, Mattio, Johnny D, Marcus, Tofty, Dan, Ricardo, Ali, Joeburg, Liz, Sinclair, Graeme, Johnny Mac (when are you coming back?), Alastair, Nina B, Chris Jermany and the rest of the good citizens of planet FP past and NAI FP present for their support and unintentional provision of material for my next project. All at HAFAD. Berkeley Menthol. The Sounds: Tom, Shirl, Catatonia, Stereophonics, Super Furries, Gene, House of America OST, Awn Ymlaen, Max Boyce 'Live' at Treorchy Rugby Club 1973.

Introduction

The best thing to come out of Wales since the Second Severn Crossing? Maybe, especially if you consider the parallels - you only have to pay on the way in. What this book primarily aims to achieve is a positive view of Wales; a celebration of the culture, an understanding of the energy and illustrations of the influence of a unique nation under a distinct groove. Written in a contemporary and accessible way, I hope this work of reference will amuse as well as inform.

I have been involved in passionate and social experimentation over the Bridge for several years. While allowing objectivity in compiling this volume, any critics of said approach would benefit from considering the words of Henry Richard MP (1812-1888):

"You knew me. You knew that though my lot was cast in London, yet I had been loyal in heart to the old land of my birth, the scene of my childhood's joys, and the place of my fathers' sepulchres; you knew that I had never missed an opportunity to do what I could to promote the religious, educational and political interests of my country; and you knew that I had done all in my power to repel the base and groundless calumnies by which our natural reputation had been defamed."

"To begin at the beginning."

(quoted from 'Under Milk Wood' by Dylan Thomas)

"It's a ghastly place. Huge gangs of tough sinewy men roam the valleys terrifying people with their close harmony singing."

(quoted from Blackadder III)

Contents

Landscape

Wales is a country of extremes, its landscape included.

It has breathtaking, climbable, mountains and sloping valleys; lofty waterfalls and deep mines; historical bridges and miles of underground caverns; expanses of water, both natural and manmade; coastal and inland walkways; ancient monuments and pioneering wind farms; National Parks, Areas of Outstanding Natural Beauty, Roman roads, award-winning beaches and outlying islands containing unique creatures and other living specimens.

Welsh history (poetic, agricultural, industrial and political) and the people who formed it, of course have left the marks of what's past and outline a template for what's to come.

The depressing decline of heavy industry which destroyed communities is now giving way to a resurgence in wildlife - the valleys are green again.

* **Pistyll Rhaeadr Waterfall**

  one of the Seven Wonders of Wales, is taller than Niagara Falls;

* **Bala Lake (Llyn Tegid)**

  is the largest natural lake in Wales;

* **Snowdon**

  dominates the landscape of north Wales, its summit is the highest peak in England and Wales at 3,560 ft (1,085 m);

* **Snowdonia Mountain Railway**

  since 1896, it has been the only public rack and pinion railway in the UK;

* **Cefn Coed Colliery**

  near Creunant, was the deepest anthracite coal mine in the world when it opened;

* **Newquay**

  on the Cardiganshire coast (yes there is another one aside from Cornwall) was a 17th and 18th century smuggling haven for wine, French brandy, tobacco, lace and even salt. Secluded inlets and coves along the shoreline concealed contraband for later distribution. It was once called a place of 'infamous notoriety';

* **Camera Obscura**

  the world's largest camera obscura sits on top of Aberystwyth's Constitution Hill and once needed adjusting to preserve the privacy of the locals;

* **Castle Density**

  in terms of architecture, Wales has more castles per square mile than any other country in Europe;

* **Largest Castle**

  Caerphilly Castle, which stands in a 30 acre site, is the largest castle in Wales and the second largest in Europe (behind Windsor);

* **Oldest Castle**

  Chepstow Castle is the oldest in the UK;

* **Largest Orangery**

  the world's largest Orangery is at Margam Abbey;

* **Largest Caravan Park**

  Trecco Bay Holiday Park at Porthcawl is Europe's largest caravan resort.

Welsh Castles

There are 170 castles in Wales. Here are 10 of the most interesting in terms of history, structure and location:

Beaumaris Castle

Caernarfon Castle

Carreg Cennen Castle

Castell Coch

Castell Dinas Bran

Chepstow Castle

Conwy Castle

Harlech Castle

Pembroke Castle

Raglan Castle

Welsh Beaches and Seaside Resorts

North Wales

Bangor

Barmouth

Colwyn Bay

Conwy

Fairbourne

Llandudno

Llanfairfechan

Penmaenmawr

Prestatyn

Rhos-on-Sea

Rhyl

Rhyme

Anglesey

Beaumaris

Cemaes Bay

Cemlyn Bay

Holyhead

Penmon

Lleyn Peninsula

Aberdaron

Abersoch

Criccieth

Hells Mouth Bay (Porth Neigwl)

Nefyn

Porthmadog

Portmeirion

Pwllheli

Tremadog Bay

Cardigan Bay

Aberaeron

Aberdyfi

Aberporth

Aberystwyth

Borth

Cwmtudu

Gwbert on Sea

Llangrannog

Mwnt

New Quay

Tresaith

Tywyn

Pembrokeshire

Broad Haven

Cilgerran

Dale

Dinas Cross

Fishguard

Freshwater East

Goodwick

Laugharne

Manorbier

Marloes

Newgale

Newport

Pembroke

Saundersfoot

Solva

St Brides Bay

St David's

Tenby

Carmarthenshire

Amroth

Cefn Sidan

Ferryside

Llansteffan

Marros

Pembrey

Pendine

St Ishmael (Kidwelly)

Swansea and Gower

Bracelet Bay

Broughton Bay

Caswell Bay

Langland

Limeslade Bay

Llangennith

Mumbles

Oxwich Bay

Port Eynon

Pwlldu Bay

Rhossili

Rotherslade

Swansea Bay

Three Cliffs Bay

Tor Bay

Whiteford Burrows

Whitford Sands

South Wales

Barry

Llantwit Major

Merthyr Mawr

Ogmore by Sea

Penarth

Porthcawl

Rhoose

Southerndown

Gardens

North Wales

Bodnant Garden

Chirk Castle

Erddig

Penrhyn Castle

Plas Newydd

Mid-Wales

Hafod

Llanerchaeron

Powis Castle

South-West Wales

Aberglasney

Clyne Gardens

Colby Woodland Garden

National Botanic Garden

Picton Castle

Plantasia

Singleton Park

South-East Wales

Gnoll Estate

Museum of Welsh Life

Tredegar Park

Roath Park

Welsh Spa Towns

Builth Wells

Llandrindod Wells

Llanwrtyd Wells

Architects of Welsh birth or extraction

John Belle

A Principal in Beyer, Blinder & Belle in New York, he is responsible for the refurbishment of Grand Central Station. The company has also renovated South Street Seaport, Ellis Island, Rockefeller Center, the Chrysler Building and New York Botanical Gardens.

Sir Clough Williams-Ellis

His most famous work is the magical, neoclassical fantasy that is Portmeirion. Based on Italy's Portofino, Portmeirion is where the famous pottery comes from and where Welsh-American architect, Frank Lloyd Wright, visited during his only ancestral field trip. He later set up the Council for the Preservation of Rural Wales which, in turn, established the three National Parks.

Frank Lloyd Wright

New York's Guggenheim Museum is one of his most famous designs and crowning achievements. He celebrated his Welsh heritage with the motto "Y Gwir yn Erbyn y Byd" ("The Truth against the World") and a bardic symbol adorns many of his buildings and works.

Nature

National Parks

* Brecon Beacons;
* Snowdonia (Eryri);
* Pembrokeshire Coast.

The purpose of the National Parks is to conserve the natural beauty, wildlife and cultural heritage of the areas in which they are situated and to provide outdoor recreation for the general public.

Areas of Outstanding Natural Beauty

* The Gower (the first area to be designated as an AONB);
* The Wye Valley;
* The Lleyn Peninsula;
* The Clwydian Range;
* The Anglesey Coast.

Island Life

The Countryside Council for Wales is the Government's statutory adviser on sustaining natural beauty, wildlife and outdoor enjoyment throughout

Wales and its inshore waters. Its remit also includes the Welsh islands where many diverse management techniques are employed by a number of different organisations and individuals to care for and preserve their ecological, geological, archaeological and cultural interests.

The Islands off North Wales

Bardsey Island

Bardsey is situated off the end of the Lleyn peninsula in north Wales and reached by boats from Aberdaron and Pwllheli. The Bardsey Island Trust bought the island in 1979 following a public appeal and in 1986 it became a National Nature Reserve.

Once a famous place of pilgrimage it is the burial place of 20,000 Saints. The ruins of the 13th century monastery tower are the remains of St Mary's Augustinian Abbey and the farmhouses on the island are listed by the Royal Commission of Ancient Monuments. One of these, Cristin, has been a Bird and Field Observatory since 1953.

Bardsey is very important for a number of seabirds including Manx shearwaters and choughs, it is also notable for its mosses, liverworts and lichens as well as flowering plants. Flat Holm is important for its maritime sward (a large area of short maritime grass) which includes an important population of the rare wild leek and bird's foot clover. The island is also renowned for its breeding populations of lesser black-backed gulls, herring gulls and shelduck and it farms mainly sheep and a small number of Welsh Black cattle.

Puffin Island

Puffin Island keeps what is considered to be the largest stand of elder scrub in the UK. The island's limestone sea cliffs and open grasslands are valuable nesting areas for many seabirds including puffins, guillemots, razorbills, shags, fulmars and the largest colony of cormorants (more than 700 pairs) in the UK. It is located just off the eastern tip of the Isle of Anglesey.

The Islands off Pembrokeshire

The estuary at the mouth the river Loughor near Llanelli is the most important in Wales (and among the ten most important in the world) in terms of the riches of its wildlife. When the Sea Empress disaster occurred off the south-west coast of Wales in 1996 it impacted on the Pembrokeshire coast's microscopic sea life, seabird breeding grounds, seals and cockles.

Caldey Island

Caldey lies within south Pembrokeshire. It is one of the UK's holy islands as the Cistercian monks (often described as Trappists) who live there continue a tradition which began on the island in Celtic times. More than a thousand years of prayer and quiet living have made this remote island a haven of peace.

The monks of Caldey follow the strict lifestyle of their order. They make vows of poverty, chastity and obedience, observe a rule of silence between 7:00 pm and 7:00 am and follow a timetable of prayer, study and work.

Grassholm Island

Grassholm is the UK's second most important gannet breeding colony, with tens of thousands of pairs. The remote habitat is also home to an RSPB bird sanctuary.

Ramsey Island

Ramsey's particular material worth is in its maritime heath which is classed as an internationally endangered habitat. The island has many rare plants including the floating water-plantain which is rare in Europe. As well as supporting seabirds in general, the island has a significant Welsh population of choughs, with eight breeding pairs recorded on the island. Just off the coast near St David's, it offers whale and dolphin watching.

Skokholm Island

Skokholm was the site of the first bird observatory in the UK, established in 1933. It is also of major importance for its breeding population of seabirds (including more than 40,000 Manx shearwaters and up to 4,000 pairs of storm petrel). It also has many rare invertebrates including 25 nationally scarce beetles.

Skomer Island

Skomer supports the largest concentration of breeding seabirds in England and Wales, including many puffins, kittiwakes, guillemots and razorbills. There is an enormous population of Manx shearwaters on Skomer - about half the world population.

Skomer is now effectively cut off from the rest of Pembrokeshire because of environmental erosion which means that predators like rats, cats, dogs and foxes are absent. This, along with restricted human traffic, is one of the major reasons for the island's importance as a breeding ground for burrow nesting seabirds and unique wildlife.

Made a National Nature Reserve, a Site of Special Scientific Interest and a Special Protection Area under European Law it has vast numbers of rabbits present and its own subspecies of Bank Vole: the Skomer Vole. Grey Seals, porpoises and dolphins can also be seen off the island.

There are no trees on the island however, only grasses such as Red Fescue and Common Bent can survive and the only edible plants that pull through are ones unpalatable to the rodents. Flowers are abundant though.

Occupation by man from the Iron Age onwards is evident: most of Skomer is an ancient monument. In the early 1800s a farmhouse was built in the centre of the island and some of the outbuildings are currently in use as accommodation for visitors and volunteers working on the island.

Nature's Notables

* The Stonehenge stones came from Pembrokeshire. They were taken by the Neolithic Beaker people from the Preseli mountains and shipped to Wiltshire to recreate the ritual power of the region;

* All three species of British woodpecker breed in Wales;

* South Gower grows the only yellow whitlow grass in the UK;

* The woods at Silent Valley near Ebbw Vale form one of the highest and most westerly natural beech woods in the UK;

* Pentrosfa Mire near Llandrindod Wells grows over 100 species of lichen including one which is new to science;

* Cors Goch near Bangor is one of a handful of sites in Wales that accommodate medicinal leeches.

Geography

Counties

Prior to April 1974

Anglesey

Brecknockshire

Caernarvonshire

Cardiganshire

Carmarthenshire

Denbighshire

Flintshire

Glamorgan

Merionethshire

Monmouthshire

Montgomeryshire

Pembrokeshire

Radnorshire

1 April 1974 to 31 March 1996 (inclusive)

Clwyd

Dyfed

Geography

Gwent

Gwynedd

Mid Glamorgan

Powys

South Glamorgan

West Glamorgan

1 April 1996 to 31 March 1997 (inclusive)

English Name	**Welsh Name**
Blaenau Gwent	Blaenau Gwent
Bridgend	Pen-y-bont ar Ogwr
Caerphilly	Caerffili
Cardiff	Caerdydd
Carmarthenshire	Sir Gaerfyrddin
Ceredigion	Sir Ceredigion
Conwy	Conwy
Denbighshire	Sir Ddinbych
Flintshire	Sir y Fflint
Gwynedd	Gwynedd
Isle of Anglesey	Sir Ynys Môn
Merthyr Tydfil	Merthyr Tudful
Monmouthshire	Sir Fynwy
Neath Port Talbot	Castell-Nedd Port Talbot

Newport	Casnewydd
Pembrokeshire	Sir Benfro
Powys	Powys
Rhondda Cynon Taff	Rhondda Cynon Tâf
Swansea	Abertawe
The Vale of Glamorgan	Bro Morgannwg
Torfaen	Tor-faen
Wrexham	Wrecsam

1 April 1997 to 31 March 1998 (inclusive)

English Name	**Welsh Name**
Blaenau Gwent	Blaenau Gwent
Bridgend	Pen-y-bont ar Ogwr
Caerphilly	Caerffili
Cardiff	Caerdydd
Carmarthenshire	Sir Gaerfyrddin
Ceredigion	Sir Ceredigion
Conwy	Conwy
Denbighshire	Sir Ddinbych
Flintshire	Sir y Fflint
Gwynedd	Gwynedd
Isle of Anglesey	Sir Ynys Môn
Merthyr Tydfil	Merthyr Tudful

Monmouthshire	Sir Fynwy
Neath Port Talbot	Castell-Nedd Port Talbot
Newport	Casnewydd
Pembrokeshire	Sir Benfro
Powys	Powys
Rhondda Cynon Taff	Rhondda Cynon Tâf
Swansea	Abertawe
The Vale of Glamorgan	Bro Morgannwg
Torfaen	Tor-faen
Wrexham	Wrecsam

1 April 1998 onwards

English Name	**Welsh Name**
Blaenau Gwent	Blaenau Gwent
Bridgend	Pen-y-bont ar Ogwr
Caerphilly	Caerffili
Cardiff	Caerdydd
Carmarthenshire	Sir Gaerfyrddin
Ceredigion	Sir Ceredigion
Conwy	Conwy
Denbighshire	Sir Ddinbych
Flintshire	Sir y Fflint
Gwynedd	Gwynedd

Isle of Anglesey	Sir Ynys Môn
Merthyr Tydfil	Merthyr Tudful
Monmouthshire	Sir Fynwy
Neath Port Talbot	Castell-Nedd Port Talbot
Newport	Casnewydd
Pembrokeshire	Sir Benfro
Powys	Powys
Rhondda Cynon Taff	Rhondda Cynon Tâf
Swansea	Abertawe
The Vale of Glamorgan	Bro Morgannwg
Torfaen	Tor-faen
Wrexham	Wrecsam

The Capital City

Cardiff became the capital city of Wales in 1955 and owes much of its history to the Industrial Revolution in the 18th century. The trade in iron and coal was a catalyst for the construction of the docks. Butetown and the surrounding docklands grew into a cosmopolitan community with some 50 nationalities settling in the area which became known as Tiger Bay.

By 1913 Cardiff docks was handling more coal than any other port in the world. Exports peaked at over 13 million tonnes (beating the nearby port at Barry which held the previous record of 11 million tonnes two years earlier). At this time the international price of coal was struck in the Coal Exchange building and it was here that the world's first £1 million deal was signed.

In 1945, 30% of the Welsh male workforce was employed in the coal and steel industries but the gradual decline in heavy industry naturally affected the area and by the early 1980s it was a relative wasteland. Enter Cardiff Bay Development Corporation. Cardiff Bay, as it is now known, has been invigorated and regenerated with new office accommodation, executive housing, entertainment and leisure facilities (including one of Wales' first 5* hotels) and is home to the world-class Wales Millennium Centre and the Welsh Assembly Government.

The city centre itself and the outlying suburbs offer similar facilities (with sport being served by the Millennium Stadium of course) with the addition of historic buildings, educational powerhouses, TV broadcasters and facilities houses, museums and a teaching hospital. The transport infrastructure continues to develop, as you would expect from a modern and cosmopolitan European capital, and from here you can easily reach the south Wales valleys and Brecon to the north, the border via two Severn crossings to the east, the Vale of Glamorgan to the west and the beginning of the fantastic coastline.

Geographical Landmarks

Offa's Dyke

Offa's Dyke ('Clawdd Offa') reaches from Prestatyn to Chepstow. It is no Iron Curtain and was never meant to be a barrier, merely an agreement between Offa and the Welsh to mark the boundary between England and the 8th century newly independent Wales. It now mostly exists as a psychological barrier but you can walk along parts of it.

Millennium Stadium

The most famous and recognisable of all Welsh landmarks at the moment is the Millennium Stadium in Cardiff. Built on the site of the world famous Cardiff Arms Park (only the North Stand of the old ground remains) the 40,000 sq m Millennium Stadium is the world's largest stadium with a retractable roof. It seats 74,500 and is almost visible from the moon.

56,000 tonnes of concrete and steel was used in its construction, the masts are the highest points in the Cardiff skyline at over 90 metres and it takes 20 minutes to open and close the roof. Its capacity includes 128 hospitality boxes, 380 wheelchair spaces and 15 public bars (many of which can deliver 12 pints in 20 seconds via their 'Joy' machines).

The first event held at the Millennium Stadium was a rugby match in June, 1999. By the 1st October the same year Cardiff was ready to host the Rugby World Cup, the final of which recorded the first £5 million gate in the history of sport in the UK.

Llanfairpwllgwyngyllgogerychwyrndrobwll llantysiliogogogoch

The station of Llanfair PG (the usual abbreviation) was the first on Anglesey, and opened in 1848. A Menai Bridge tailor is credited with the modification of the name in the 1880s. It was intended as a tongue-in-cheek publicity stunt to attract traffic and tourists to the island and was, for many years, the longest station name in the UK until a nearby upstart got in on the act. Llanfairpwllgwyngyllgogerychwyrndrobwll llantysiliogogogoch remains the longest official place-name in the UK and 3rd in the world.

It literally translates as:

Llanfair - pwllgwyngyll - gogerychwyrndrobwll - llantysilio - gogogoch

The Church of St Mary - in the hollow of the white hazel - near the fierce whirlpool - and the Church of St Tysilio - by the red cave.

Geographical Points of Note

* Blaenavon, with its Big Pit Mining Museum, is a World Heritage Site;

* Blaenau Ffestiniog's Llechwedd Slate Caverns runs underground tram rides;

* Sir Malcolm Campbell broke the World Land Speed Record in 1925, when he averaged 146.16 mph, at Pendine on the Pembrokeshire coast;

* Rupert the Bear's adventures were set in Beddgelert;

* Peter Rabbit's garden was in Tenby.

Economy

The long traditions of what the Welsh economy was built on: mining, agriculture and manufacture are giving way to more modern and diverse occupations. The Welsh have had to diversify and manage change constructively, especially during the last 25 years, in order to not only survive but flourish.

Wales is continuing to move away from dependence on basic commodity production to activities which call for greater levels of skill and knowledge. Achieving the crucial conversion is central to developing economic prosperity. For example, farms are diversifying in order to offer holiday accommodation, former mining communities are turning to tourism opportunities and many people are becoming their own bosses running their own businesses in the fields of media and information technology. Wales' flagship social enterprise, Tower Colliery, operates as a co-operative enterprise owned and managed by the miners themselves.

Promoting the social economy is one of the main objectives of the Welsh Development Agency (WDA). A Welsh Assembly Government sponsored body, the WDA's work involves supporting and developing social enterprises with regenerating local communities. A new engineering centre in Port Talbot following the steel industry crisis is an example of their impact and Objective One money now flowing in from Europe is treating the economy holistically - targeting the most disadvantaged areas first.

Business

Business People

Howard Marks

International enigma: hippy, narcotic smuggler, black marketeer, prisoner, drinker of raindeer urine. At his zenith in the mid-1980s he is said to have had 43 aliases, 89 phone lines and 25 companies. The most colourful, famous and formidably hard to find drug smuggler from Kenfig Hill expressed an interest in becoming the first UK Drug Tzar which was panned by the government.

Sir Terry Matthews

Wales' first billionaire. He invested hundreds of millions of pounds turning the former nursing home where he was born in Newport, Gwent, into the 5* Celtic Manor Resort - Europe's leading conference resort, home of the Wales Open and the venue for the 2010 Ryder Cup.

Charles Stewart Rolls

One half of Rolls-Royce, the luxury car makers, was originally from Monmouth.

Businesses and Organisations

Rachel's Organic Dairy

Founded by Gareth and Rachel Rowlands, their Brynllys farm near Aberystwyth was the first and now fastest growing, certified organic dairy in the UK. It has the longest continuous record of organic production, persisting with the pioneering origins of the family business established in 1942.

The Rowlands took on the farm in 1966, selling their milk to the Milk Marketing Board (MMB). By the early 1980s worries about the effects of milk quotas on the farm made them want to make changes. Events overtook them, however, as the severe winter snow storms of 1982 prevented tankers from collecting their milk. As the farm was completely snowed in Rachel conceived the idea of producing yogurt, resurrecting her grandmother's recipe book.

The demand from local shops and hotels together with the zeitgeist for organic produce from UK consumers in general has seen all the major supermarkets such as Sainsbury's, Waitrose, Tesco and Safeway, as well as independent retailers, stocking Rachel's Organic Dairy products. In addition, Rachel Rowlands is now an MBE.

Tenovus

The Tenovus cancer charity was set up in 1943 by ten businessmen ('ten-of-us') and now invests around £2 million each year on cancer research, education patient care and counselling.

Cardiff businessman Eddie Price was the inspiration for the venture during a hospital stay. The support of his nine friends equipped the beds of the Cardiff Royal Infirmary, where he was recovering, with radio headsets. This gesture became the basis for forming the charity.

Tenovus' legacy includes funding the first fully equipped Spina Bifida Unit of its kind in the world and developing the drug Tamoxifen, acknowledged as one of the most important treatments for breast cancer.

Companies House

The UK has employed a system of company registration since 1844. All limited companies in the UK are registered at Companies House, an Executive Agency of the Department of Trade and Industry, in Cardiff. More than 1.8 million limited companies are registered there and 300,000+ new companies are incorporated each year.

DVLA

The Driver and Vehicle Licensing Agency is an Executive Agency of the Department for Transport (DfT) with the primary aims of facilitating road safety, collecting vehicle excise duty (car tax) and maintaining registers of drivers and vehicles.

In the 1960s when vehicles were sold, or keepers moved house, logbook details had to be transferred from one area to another. The system in place at the time could not cope with the millions of documents passing backwards and forwards. Therefore, in 1965, the Government decided that a new system should be introduced. Central administration with automatic data processing was created along with the Driver and Vehicle Licensing Centre (DVLC). Based in Swansea, it was the forerunner [sorry] of the DVLA.

Royal Mint

The British Royal Mint, where Sterling is produced, is an Executive Agency of the government. It has maintained its position as the world's leading exporting Mint from its base at Llantrisant - sometimes described as "the hole with the Mint in it".

Edwards Millions/Manhattan Millions

New York's Manhattan is arguably Welsh-owned. Hundreds of Welsh families have been involved in repeated attempts at litigation, claiming back rent from Manhattan since the 19th century.

Billions of dollars are said to be owing to descendants of Robert Edwards who was allegedly given the land that Manhattan is built on by the Crown.

It is claimed that the land was then leased out and that the lease later expired but the Edwards Millions are disputed by Trinity Church, which says it was granted the land by Queen Anne in 1705.

DNA testing is now being utilised in the claim, which doesn't appear to be anywhere near a settlement as very little documentary evidence exists.

Business First

The 'terribly geeky' list of movies created by Cardiff University students including Col Needham, thanks to the World Wide Web circa 1993, became an irresistible catalogue of who/what/when for cinema. The Cardiff Movie Database soon changed from a labour of love to a commercial venture. A name change followed and the Internet Movie Database (IMDb.com) was one of three websites acquired by Amazon.com in a $55 million deal in 1998.

History

Gerald of Wales (Giraldus Cambrensis) was an early chronicler of Welsh culture and politics whose words, scripted for the interest of Latin scholars, still resonate in the ripened contemporary subject of his reporting.

Kings and Princes

King Arthur

Arthur's name first appears in early Welsh texts and he was based at Caerleon - so the Welsh claimed him as one of their own. His life was mythological yet everybody knows about the pulling of the sword from a stone, the Round Table, Merlin, The Lady of the Lake, Excalibur, the Holy Grail and Camelot.

When given the option of printing the truth or the legend always print the legend.

Llywelyn ap Iorwerth

Llywelyn ap Iorwerth inherited a third of the ancient kingdom of Gwynedd and by the time he reached 27 was the most powerful figure in north Wales. His politicking thrust him south, capturing Powys and Ceredigion on the way. The 1218 Treaty of Worcester recognised him as the single most powerful figure in Wales at the time.

Wales' laws were refined under Llywelyn ap Iorwerth which his grandson, Llywelyn ap Gruffudd, would later develop.

Llywelyn ap Gruffudd

A dignified leader yet uncompromising in battle Llywelyn Ein Llyw Olaf (The Last Prince), as he became known, was the only Welshman ever to be recognised as Prince of Wales by a King of England.

Between 1258 and 1277 destiny seemed to be hinting at Welsh independence, the architect of this lot was Llewelyn ap Gruffudd. He was killed in 1282 though along with any real hope of Welsh autonomy for another 700 years.

Owain Lawgoch

There were two Princes of Wales fighting on opposite sides in mid-14th century France. One was (officially) the Black Prince, the other was (psychologically) Owain ap Thomas ap Rhodri. The great nephew of Llywelyn II declared himself Prince of Gwynedd during the Hundred Years War but swings and roundabouts finally saw him assassinated at the siege of Mortagne in 1378, ending his vivid career and the entire line of Wales' most prestigious royal house.

Owain Glyndŵr (sometimes anglicised to Owen Glendower)

An early guerrilla; defender of freedom, a Welsh church independent from England and self-rule.

A cultivated man (he was "exceeding well read"

according to Shakespeare) Owain Glyndŵr appears an unlikely rebel considering his background, connections and education. By 1400 though he was a natural leader for his discontented countrymen inciting a national uprising, proclaiming himself Prince of Wales and exalting the national conscience for a new Parliament in Machynlleth in 1404.

Always elusive he would retreat into his heartland when in trouble; evading capture, sharpening his military tactics, ensuring his legendary status remained intact and creating the template for future guerrilla leaders. In fact, Che Guevara is said to have been influenced by the Welsh rebel and Fidel Castro claims to have a book on his life in his study.

Henry Tudor (VII)

The Welsh-speaking King of England who set about reducing the power of the nobility. His claim to the English throne came via his mother's membership of the House of Lancaster and the Tudors put an end to the subjugation that Wales and the Welsh had borne for centuries.

Politics

Political Context

The first Minister of Welsh Affairs appointed by Churchill following the establishment of the Ministry of Welsh Affairs in 1951 was Sir David Maxwell-Fyfe. He was given the epithet 'Dai Bananas' by the Welsh as they saw this move, rather than providing them with an ambassador and an early attempt at devolution, as an avenue to erode the Liberal presence at the time in Wales.

When Wales went to the polls on the question of devolution on St David's Day in 1979 the result was an overwhelming 'No' to a Welsh Assembly. However, after 18 years of Conservative rule Labour was returned to power and devolution was back on the agenda. On 18 September 1997 another referendum was held and a dramatic night returned a very slender majority of 6,721 votes in favour. Finally it was 'Yes for Wales' ('Ie Dros Gymru').

It represented a remarkable shift of voter opinion for which Ron Davies can take much of the credit. He steered the Government of Wales Act through Parliament and successfully delivered devolution to Wales which provided for the powers of the London-appointed Secretary of State for Wales to be transferred to a directly elected National Assembly in Cardiff. Ron Davies was therefore destined to be First Secretary of the National Assembly for Wales, but the beginning of his career suicide was assured following an incident he described as a "moment of madness" on Clapham Common in 1998.

Today, the National Assembly for Wales consists of 60 Members with many of its powers in the hands of the First Minister who leads the National Assembly Government.

Famous Politicians

Aneurin ('Nye') Bevan -Tredegar

Ron Davies - Caerphilly

Lord Dafydd Elis-Thomas - Carmarthen

Gwynfor Evans - Barry

Michael Foot (former MP for Ebbw Vale) - Plymouth

David Lloyd George (former Prime Minister) - Manchester

Megan Lloyd George - Criccieth

Keir Hardie (former MP for Merthyr Tydfil) - Scotland

Michael Heseltine - Swansea

Michael Howard - Llanelli

Sir Geoffrey Howe (Lord Howe) - Penycae

Roy Jenkins - Abersychan

Neil Kinnock - Tredegar

Rhodri Morgan - Cardiff

John Prescott - Prestatyn

George Thomas (Viscount Tonypandy) - Port Talbot

Population/ Demographics

Population

2,903,085

Geographical Spread

22% of the population were born in Wales but live in England.

Ethnicity

97.88% describe themselves as white.

A diverse mix of cultures exists, particularly around the major towns and cities. People with ethnic backgrounds other than white are concentrated in the the three biggest cities of Cardiff, Swansea and Newport. These three combined also accommodate 2/3rds of the total population (307,000).

Religion

Faith

72% of the population is Christian followed by Islam. Less than 1% describe themselves as Muslim, next come Indian Hindus, White Buddhists, White Jews and Indian Sikhs.

Howell Harris

Howell Harris was at the helm of the 18th century Methodist Revival following an epiphany in Talgarth Church. The schoolmaster and compulsive diarist from Trefeca had, as confirmed by his tombstone, "tasted grace" so he was resolved to becoming an itinerant preacher evangelising far and wide despite toothache, piles and gout.

Wales was fertile ground for the spread of Methodism and Howell Harris' vigour was assisted by the inability of the Anglican hierarchy to speak Welsh - still the language of the masses at the time.

Thomas Charles

A successor to Howell Harris, Rev Thomas Charles aimed to provide Bibles for his entire congregation. So moved was he that a young girl called Mary Jones walked barefoot the 30 or so miles to Bala to procure a Welsh Bible that he founded the Welsh Sunday School movement in Wales and the British and Foreign Bible Society.

Archbishop Rowan Williams

The Archbishop of Canterbury, Rowan Williams, is a Welsh-speaking Welshman from Ystradgynlais. The youngest professor at Oxford University has become a vocal advocate for the ordination of women and openly homosexual bishops.

Culture & Language

In his influential 1958 book Culture and Society Welshman Raymond Williams redefined culture as a much wider phenomenon than it had previously been perceived. Popular culture - he argued - was every bit as valid as the intellectual. His ideas hinted at the acceptance of mass entertainment forms like pop music, television and film as subjects for serious critical appraisal. A whole new discipline was born, Cultural Studies, and it is thanks to him that books like this one have a place.

Wales is rich in culture and traditions - having its own language and cultural events famous throughout the world.

Language

"You need half a pint of phlegm in your throat just to pronounce the place names. Never ask for directions in Wales, you'll be washing spit out of your hair for a fortnight." (quoted from Blackadder III)

Origins of the Welsh Language

The Celtic languages have their roots around the 6th century. Inside the Roman areas Celtic languages were effected to degrees by Latin: leading the the development of Welsh, Cornish and Breton which are all closely related. The Welsh are in fact an Anglo-Saxon invention - from 'weala(s)' meaning 'foreigner(s)'.

The Welsh Bible

Bishop William Morgan from Penmachno saved the Welsh language. He was priest of several northern parishes before becoming Bishop of Llandaff and later Bishop of St Asaph.

The 1536 and 1542-1543 Acts of Union forbade the use of Welsh in public life and sought to make English the 'official' language of Wales. However, a consequence of the threat of Spanish invasion saw a further Act passed in 1563 which allowed the Scriptures and the Book of Common Prayer to be translated into Welsh insuring against the Welsh turning Catholic.

William Morgan was well placed to translate the Bible into Welsh as his education had included the study of both Hebrew and Greek - the original languages of the Bible. The translation was published in 1588, the same year the Spanish Armada sailed for the UK.

The William Morgan Bible was significant in that it was written in a classic, literary style and used to teach successive generations how to read, write and speak good Welsh - the power of its language playing a central role as the basis for the modern Welsh that is spoken today.

Renaissance of the Welsh Language

Today, the Celtic languages are considered minority languages but of these Welsh is the strongest and most widely spoken with 600,000+ speaking it in Wales alone (Census 2001). Agencies like 'Bwrdd yr Iaith Gymraeg' (The Welsh Language Board) and 'Cymdeithas yr Iaith' (The Welsh Language Society) are behind this revival in the language.

The Welsh Language Described

Welsh is a phonemic language and largely phonetic (what you see is what you get). This, told as seen, facet of the language gives those unfamiliar with it the ability to pronounce the written word relatively easily. There are no, for example, silent letters to struggle with; only the stress occurring mostly on the last syllable of words or where the circumflex (ˆ), grave accents (`) and (´) or umlaut (¨) are present.

There are some slight variations in the way the language is spoken in different parts of the country. For example, dialects dictate that milk is expressed as 'llefrith' in the north and 'llaeth' in the south, similarly keys are 'agoriadau' in the north and 'allweddi' in the south and sweets are 'fferins' in the north and 'losin' in the south.

The only other basic considerations in the structure of the language to take on board are that mutations occur to some initial letters of words to make them softer and easier to pronounce, words are either masculine or feminine and that two forms of address exist - formal and informal.

Mutations

Details of which consonants mutate and how they are affected.

The Soft Mutation

P > B
T > D
C > G
B > F
D > Dd
G > (gets dropped)
Ll > L
Rh > R
M > F

The Nasal Mutation

P > MH
T > NH
C > NGH
B > M
D > N
G > NG

The Aspirate Mutation

P > PH
T > TH
C > CH

Tongue Twisters

To have a go at the language, try these tongue-twisters. This is just for fun but you may need to clear away any delicate objects from your surroundings and keep anyone with/near you a safe distance away.

lladd dafad ddall

killing a blind sheep

hwch goch a chwech cochion bach

a red sow and six small red ones

Llanfairpwllgwyngyllgogerychwyrndrobwllllantysi liogogogoch

Llanfair PG (The Anglesey Train Station)

The Welsh Alphabet

A B C CH D Dd E F Ff G Ng H I L
Ll M N O P Ph R Rh S T Th U W Y

a b c ch d dd e f ff g ng h i l ll m n o p ph r rh s t th u w y

Notice the absence of 'J'. James and Jones are very popular surnames in Wales and likely explanations for this quirk is that John and Ieuan have become corrupted and that 'Siâm(s)' and 'Siôn' have been anglicised over the years. Joan of Arc, for example, in Welsh is 'Siân d'Arc'.

Welsh surnames are generally patronymic i.e. derived from the father's name and a relic of 'ap' ('son of'). Therefore many surnames either begin 'b' or 'p':

ap Owen = Bowen

ap Hugh/Huw = Pugh/Puw

ap Howell = Powell

ap Robert = Probert

The Vowels

A E I O U W Y + sometimes H

a e i o u w y + sometimes h

Numbers

1 One - Un

2 Two - Dau

3 Three - Tri

4 Four - Pedwar

5 Five - Pump

6 Six - Chwech

7 Seven - Saith

8 Eight - Wyth

9 Nine - Naw

10 Ten - Deg

50 Fifty - Pum deg/Hanner Cant

100 Hundred - Cant

1,000 Thousand - Mil

Days of the Week

Monday - dydd Llun

Tuesday - dydd Mawrth

Wednesday - dydd Mercher

Thursday - dydd Iau

Friday - dydd Gwener

Saturday - dydd Sadwrn

Sunday - dydd Sul

Months of the Year

January - Ionawr

February - Chwefror

March - Mawrth

April - Ebrill

May - Mai

June - Mehefin

July - Gorffennaf

August - Awst

September - Medi

October - Hydref

November - Tachwedd

December - Rhagfyr

The Seasons

The Spring - Y Gwanwyn

The Summer - Yr Haf

The Autumn - Yr Hydref

The Winter - Y Gaeaf

Bank Holidays and Calendar Markers (Pagan or Otherwise)

New Year's Eve - Nos Galan

New Year's Day - Dydd Calan

Good Friday - Dydd Gwener y Groglith

Palm Sunday - Sul y Blodau

Easter Monday - Dydd Llun y Pasg

May Day - Calan Mai

Spring Bank Holiday - Gŵyl Banc y Gwanwyn

August Bank Holiday - Gŵyl Banc Awst

Halloween - Calan Gaeaf

Bonfire Night - Noson Tân Gwyllt

Christmas Eve - Noswyl Nadolig

Christmas Day - Dydd Nadolig

Boxing Day - Gŵyl San Steffan

Specific Welsh Reasons to be Cheerful

25 January

St Dwynwen's Day - Gŵyl Santes Dwynwen [the patron saint of Welsh lovers. Draws a parallel with St Valentine.]

1 March

St David's Day - Dydd Gŵyl Dewi [the patron saint of Wales.]

Welsh Derivatives

There are some English words with a Welsh provenance. For example:

Corgi

('dwarf dog') either of two breeds of short-legged dogs, originally from Wales

[cor = dwarf + ci = dog]

Cromlech

('arched stone') a megalithic chamber tomb or dolmen; standing stone

[crom/crwm = arched + llech = flat stone/slate]

Cwm

('a valley') a deep rounded hollow with a steep side formed by a glacier; a cirque

[valley]

Eisteddfod

('session') a festival of poetry, singing and music; a congress of Welsh bards and minstrels; a national or local festival for music and poetic competitions

[eistedd = to sit]

Flummery

a pudding made with coagulated wheat flour or

oatmeal; a sweet dish made with beaten eggs; mere flattery or nonsense; empty compliments; trifles

Gorsedd

('throne') a council/meeting of bards and druids, preliminary to an eisteddfod

[throne]

Hwyl

an emotional quality inspiring impassioned eloquence; emotional fervour, characteristic of poetry recitation

[enjoyment; mood; (boat) sail; singsong; cadence]

Sayings

Cymru am Byth

Wales Forever

Iechyd Da

An expression of good wishes before taking a drink - equivalent to cheers or bottoms up. Literally means good health.

*Cnychu**

Fuck

Cnycha Bant/Cnychu Bant*

Fuck off

Diawl/Y Diawl

Devil/The Devil

Ych a Fi/Ach a Fi

Yuck

Uffern

Hell

Uffern Dân

Hell Fire

Codi pais wedi pisio*

Equivalent to 'closing the stable door after the horse has bolted'. Literally means to lift your petticoat after taking a piss i.e. pointless.

Mae croen dy din ar dy dalcen

Literal translation - the skin of your backside is on your forehead. Great - it sounds seriously insulting unless you've been trying out some dodgy

---

* Caveat - these words should merely be considered for reference purposes if you come across them in the field. Otherwise treat with extreme caution and only use them yourself if legitimately and sufficiently aroused to do so!

sexual practice, in which case could be considered quite an achievement. So, what does it mean? It is a cumbersome way of describing someone as simply tired. Much more interesting though is the suggestion that finding the skin of your arse on your forehead reveals that you've had your head so far up it you have come away with incontrovertible evidence. Thus, you are pretentious and/or ignorant.

Un Wennol Ni Wna Wanwyn

Tricky this one as it translates 'one swallow does not make spring'. It's tricky because in the company of English speakers the phrase is 'one swallow does not a summer make' so a diatribe is always sparked as to which season the swallow isn't forecasting.

Glossary of Welsh Place-Names

This is a list explaining Welsh place-name derivatives. English spellings of Welsh cities, towns and villages have been offered purely for reference purposes and to provide basic examples. Those cities, towns and villages that also exist in English with different spellings are rendered in italics.

aber - mouth of a river, confluence [Aberaeron/ Abergavenny/Aberporth/Abersoch/Aberystwyth]

bedd - grave [Beddau/Beddgelert]

bryn - hill [Brynamman/Brynsiencyn]

caer - fort [Caerleon/Caernarvon]

capel - chapel [Capel Curig/Capel Iwan]

castell - castle [*Castell-nedd*]

coed - trees, wood [*Y Coed Duon*]

cwm - valley [Cwmllynfell/Cwmtudu/Cwmtwrch]

dinas - city [Dinas Cross/Dinas Mallwyd]

dol - meadow [Dolau/Dolgellau/Dolwyddelan]

eglwys - church [Eglwysfach/Eglwyswrw]

ffos - ditch, trench - [Ffostrasol]

glan - bank, shore [Glanaethwy/Glanllwyd]

glyn - vale, glen [Glyndyfrdwy/*Glyn Ebwy*]

hafod - summer dwelling place [Hafod Wen]

hen - old [Hendy Gwyn ar Daf]

hendre - winter dwelling place [Hendrefoelan/ Henllan]

llan - church, parish, village. Often followed by a saint's name [Llandaff/Llanfairfechan/Llanpumsaint/ Llantrisant]

maen - stone [Maenclochog/Maentwrog]

maes - field [Maesteg]

melin/felin - mill [Felinfach/Felinfoel]

nant - brook, stream [Nantycaws/Nantyglo]

pant - valley [Pantycelyn/Pantyfedwen]

pen - end, head [Penmachno/Penuwch]

pentre - village [Pentregroes/Pentre Ifan]

pont - bridge [Pont Abraham/Ponterwyd/ Pontrhydygroes/Pontypool/Pontypridd]

porth - door, port, harbour [*Porthaethwy*/ Porthmadog]

pwll - pit, pool [Pwllheli]

tre/*tref*/*dre*/*dref* - town [Trefdraeth/Trefeglwys/ Tregaron/*Y Drenewydd*]

ynys - island [Ynyshir/Ynyslas]

ystrad - vale [Ystradgynlais/Ystradowen]

Other elements which form Welsh place-names include:

afon - river

bach/fach - small

bwlch - gap, pass

cae - field

carreg/cerrig - stone, stones

coch/goch - red

cors - bog, fen

craig/graig - rock

croes/groes - cross

du/ddu - black

gwyn/wyn/wen - white

llyn - lake

mawr/fawr - big

morfa - bog, fen

mynydd/fynydd - mountain

plas - palace, mansion

rhaeadr - waterfall

rhiw - hill

rhyd - ford

sarn - causeway

tŷ - house

Motoring Language Anecdotes

Road Sign

Prior to devolution when the Welsh Office was still the Welsh Office they installed a sign on an approach road to Cardiff city centre (M4, Junction 32, aka Coryton Roundabout) announcing some impending roadworks. An innocent and everyday occurrence you may be thinking. However, the sign read "Cynllwyn gan y Swyddfa Gymreig......". Rather than being a "Plan by the Welsh Office......" to do whatever they were doing, as was of course the intention, the sign foretold of a 'conspiracy'. 'Cynllyn' is Welsh for plan and not 'cynllwyn' as appeared. This 'conspiracy' of the administration of the day to improve a Welsh road made it into Private Eye and was apparently the mistake of the Coventry based sign writers responsible.

Learner Driver

Although Welsh is recognised as an official language in Wales only very recently a learner driver, after much legal negotiation, managed to successfully appeal against a conviction for not displaying their 'L' plates. Having been displaying 'D' plates ('dysgwr' being Welsh for 'learner') they of course felt legitimately within the law.

Uniquely Welsh

Sealyham Terrier

A short-legged, wire-haired, breed of terrier with a medium length white coat. Often shortened to Sealyham as it takes its name from the village in south-west Wales that first bred it in the 19th century.

Welsh

Of or relating to Wales or its people, language or culture.

A white long-bodied, lop-eared, breed of pig primarily kept for bacon.

Welsh Black

One of the UK's oldest cattle breeds, the Welsh Blacks are now to be found overseas including the USA, Canada, Australia, New Zealand and Germany.

Welsh Cob

A breed of pony and cob renowned for their versatility, superior performance, hardiness and kind nature. Their breeding is divided into four 'Sections': Section A (Welsh Mountain Pony), Section B (Welsh Pony), Section C (Welsh Pony [Cob Type]) and Section D (Welsh Cob).

Welsh Corgi

The full name for corgi - a short-legged breed of

dog with a fox like head [comes from the Welsh 'cor' meaning dwarf + 'ci' meaning dog i.e. short/dwarf dog].

Welsh Dresser

A type of dresser. A Welsh dresser comprises a sideboard with drawers, open display shelves and storage cupboards below.

Welsh Flannel

A fine kind of flannel made from the fleece of the flocks of the Welsh mountains, and largely manufactured by hand.

Welsh Glaive, or Welsh Hook

A weapon of war used in former times by the Welsh, commonly regarded as a kind of poleaxe.

Welsh Harp

A type of harp in which the strings are arranged in three rows [used especially for the accompaniment of singing and poetry].

Welshman's Button

An angler's name for a species of caddis fly.

Welsh Mortgage

A type of mortgage, being a conveyance of an estate, redeemable at any time on payment of the principal, with an understanding that the profits in the meantime shall be received by the mortgagee without account, in satisfaction of interest.

Welsh Mountain

A common breed of small hardy sheep kept mainly in the mountains of Wales.

Welsh Mountain Pony

A small, sturdy, but graceful breed of pony used mostly for riding, originally from Wales.

Welsh Mutton

A choice and delicate kind of mutton obtained from a breed of small sheep in Wales.

Welsh Onion

A kind of onion forming clusters of bulbs, having hollow inflated stalks and leaves, but scarcely any bulb. A native of Siberia it is said to have been introduced from Germany, and is supposed to have derived its name from a German term for 'foreign'.

Welsh Parsley

Hemp, or halters made from hemp.

Welsh Poppy

A perennial western European papaveraceous plant, like a poppy but with large yellow flowers, abundant in mid-Wales.

Welsh Rarebit

Originally Welsh Rabbit but has become known as Welsh Rarebit by way of 18th century folk etymology. A savoury dish of melted cheese and seasoning (sometimes mixed with milk) served on toast.

Welsh Sheepdog

The Welsh sheepdog has a distinctive red colour and is recognised, as distinguishable from the border collie, as a hard-working animal with plenty of stamina. Threatened with extinction a decade ago, Welsh sheepdogs are now being exported around the world.

Welsh Terrier

A wire-haired breed of terrier with a black and tan coat.

Cultural Traditions

Eisteddfod (Origins)

Iolo Morgannwg (Edward Williams) was born in Llancarfan in the county which is now known as the Vale of Glamorgan (Glamorgan being the English for 'Morgannwg'). He was a stonemason by trade and once wrote 14 verses in the name of the medieval poet Dafydd ap Gwilym and sent them off for inclusion in a literary collection.

He claimed that a unique metre was in use by the bards of Glamorgan and also asserted that they would gather together in an elaborate ceremonial event that he called the 'Gorsedd' (Throne) and that the tradition had continued unbroken in Glamorgan since before the birth of Christ.

In 1792 he succeeded in persuading a number of the London Welsh to hold a 'Gorsedd' at Primrose Hill. It was 27 years later that he managed to interest the National Eisteddfod in the 'Gorsedd' and it now forms the cultural festival's three prime ceremonies. "Truth Against the World."

Eisteddfod (Modern)

Cardigan was the site of the first ever eisteddfod in 1176 and its 800th anniversary was celebrated at the National Eisteddfod of 1976. The modern annual National Eisteddfod has 19th century roots and has evolved into an annual celebration of Welsh culture, tradition and language. 'Eisteddfod' is a derivative of the Welsh 'eistedd' meaning 'to sit' (and thereby tying in with the 'Gorsedd' ceremony as outlined above). Eisteddfod is strictly defined as a congress of Welsh bards but has become a national or local festival of music, poetry, drama, art and dance.

In Wales particularly, as the eisteddfodic tradition is widespread, the Welsh culture is celebrated around a central pavilion where competitions in the above arts take place. The climax of the weeklong contest culminates in the three 'Gorsedd' ceremonies. These are the Crowning Ceremony to honour the finest free verse poet, the Chairing Ceremony for strict metre poetry and the Prose Medal Ceremony. During these ceremonies, members of the Gorsedd of Bards gather on the Eisteddfod stage in their ceremonial robes along with the Archdruid who addresses the audience.

The Urdd National Eisteddfod (organised by 'Urdd Gobaith Cymru') is a similar celebration, held separately, for the children.

St David's Day

Any or all of the traditional recipes mentioned in this book can be taken with a saliferous handful at the beginning of March every year. Dewi Sant (St David) is patron saint of Wales and the reason school children get togged up on 1st March, St David's Day, and conduct mini eisteddfods. It is still not recognised as a national holiday but nevertheless a chance to trawl for a shawl, bonnet or tall black hat, petticoat, wool skirt and a pini in the dressing up box. A leek or daffodil does suffice for the boys and adults as a lapel accoutrement as they remain symbols of Welsh independence.

Born in Ceredigion, St David studied in Aberaeron and is also believed to have studied under St Illtud at Llantwit Major. He became a prominent figure in the Celtic Church and founded a monastic community in Pembrokeshire - where the famous 12th century St David's Cathedral now stands. His most famous feat occurred at Llanddewibrefi where he addressed a prodigious gathering of his peers and the ground is said to have risen up beneath his feet creating a pulpit from which to project his words.

Love Spoons

Traditionally it was customary to give your love or the object of your desire a love spoon. These spoons were carved by hand in a shape expressing the desire of the outcome. For example, some had balls inside the handle suggesting the wish to have children. Love spoons are still presented today but are mostly bought from shops ready crafted.

Nos Galan

'Nos Galan' and 'Dydd Calan' are the Welsh names for New Year's Eve and New Year's Day respectively. As the Celtic people believed that life was a continuous circle 'Y Fari Lwyd' (the skull of a horse covered in white cloth and decorated with ribbons) comes back to life at this time, and is still paraded through some Welsh villages.

Nos Galan Races

Traditional Nos Galan (New Year's Eve) Races commemorate the legend of Guto Nyth Bran.

Griffith Morgan came from Nyth Bran Farm in the Rhondda valley in 1700. He became known as 'Guto Nyth Bran' because of his skill in catching a bird in flight and running to Pontypridd and back, some seven miles, before a (pre-electric) kettle boiled.

When he was 37, a challenge came from the 'Prince' of Bedwas to run the 12 miles from Newport in Monmouthshire to Bedwas Church near Caerphilly. Guto easily won the race, but his body gave way to the celebratory slaps on the back and he died in the arms of his sweetheart Siân. His body now resides in the graveyard of Llanwynno Church near Mountain Ash and the 5 km Nos Galan Races, started in 1958, are held in his memory.

Calennig

Another New Year's Day custom is that of 'calennig' (New Year's gift). In many Welsh villages, the boys would knock on neighbours' doors carrying three legged totems, singing rhymes and splashing them with water. This was done in positive spirit to elicit a small gift from the people of the house. Today, the custom is remembered by many Welsh households. Using 'calennig' decorations, consisting mainly of whole oranges pierced with cloves and standing on a tripod of twigs, they infuse the spirit of the past.

Identity

National identity is strong with 67% reporting their nationality as Welsh. Welsh identity is strongest in Merthyr Tydfil with the highest proportion of the total population of Wales (85%) describing themselves thus (although a media campaign at the time of the 2001 Census most certainly will have influenced both statistics).

National Emblems

The Welsh Flag

The Welsh flag is a distinctive passant red dragon on a background of two equal horizontal green and white stripes. It is said that the distinguishing mark of the dragon first appeared in Roman times, is shown on the Bayeux tapestry and was appropriated by the Tudors. 'Y Ddraig Goch' ('The Red Dragon') remains a symbol of national independence.

Leek

A vegetable with flat overlapping leaves forming an elongated cylindrical bulb, used as food. It is because of its significance as a food in the traditional Welsh diet that the leek has became a national symbol. St David adopted it, Shakespeare wrote about it and the Tudors supplied their household guards with them for St David's Day.

Daffodil

A bulbous plant of the genus Narcissus, with yellow flowers having a large trumpet-shaped corona. The origins of its use as a national symbol are patchy. It is most likely that the flower became associated with Wales because of its close resemblance to the word leek in Welsh. 'Cenhinen/cennin' is Welsh for leek(s) and 'cenhinen/Cennin Pedr' is Welsh for daffodil(s).

Prince of Wales Feathers

The crest of three ostrich feathers and the motto 'Ich Dien' (I Serve) were apparently adopted by the Black Prince at the Battle of Crecy and influenced by the King of Bohemia who led the cavalry against the English.

The Welsh Abroad

We're not talking stereotypes on a package holiday but emigrants and settlers who have made a lasting impression of a different sort.

St Patrick

St Patrick was Welsh. A south Wales mining village, Banwen in the Dulais Valley, claims St Patrick as a former resident. Many historians and historical accounts relate that he was captured as a teenager by Irish slavers and shipped over the water.

Patagonia

During the 19th century industrialisation and urbanisation that threatened the demise of the Welsh language 153 men, women and children embarked on a journey across the Atlantic. Arriving in 1865 aboard the Mimosa they colonised the first land they reached in southern Argentina because of its sheer remoteness (Palestine had been considered previously).

Congregationalist minister and theologian Michael D Jones had proposed an entirely Welsh settlement and 'Y Wladfa' (colony/settlement) was established along with towns evocative of home: Puerto Madryn, Trelew and Dolavon. Subsequent generations moved on to Chile where the landscape, including breathtaking waterfalls and vegetation are much more akin to the Welsh landscape.

Today the region carries on the tradition of the eisteddfod, welcomes regular visiting teachers of Welsh (many now funded by the National Assembly Government) and entertains student exchanges. Spanish influences are natural of course and the quirk of two colliding cultures has birthed children with hybrid names like Pablo Jenkins and Juan Jones in the farmhouses and teashops flying the Welsh flag.

America

The influence of the Welsh in America is not well-known or understood. The Irish heritage is well documented, but for centuries the Welsh have emigrated to the United States in search of prosperity and made a substantial contribution to modern American society.

Richard Amerik was the chief customs official in late 15th century Bristol and America was apparently named after him as a thank you for being the principal investor in John Cabot's transatlantic expedition of 1497. Fast forward a year to when the Florentine navigator Amerigo Vespucci landed in South America and the cartographer Martin Waldseemüller credited him with the same. Observers have drawn their own conclusions for centuries; the most egalitarian of these is that Richard Amerik gave is name to North America and Amerigo Vespucci to South (otherwise we would have been left with a continent called 'Vespuccia').

Rowland Ellis lead fellow Quakers in the 17th century to Pennsylvania from Bryn Mawr farm in Dolgellau. A replica of the farm gave its name to a town there. Families of Welsh extraction remain in Pennsylvania and similarly there is a Bethesda in

Maryland. There is also evidence of a Cardiff in New Jersey and a suburb called 'Welsh' in Los Angeles.

Between a third and a half of the signatories of the Declaration of Independence were of Welsh extraction, Thomas Jefferson's father was a north Walian and both Chief Justice Marshall and Chief Justice Charles Evans Hughes had Welsh origins. On the flip side Al Capone's accountant, a Llewelyn (Murray the Hump) Humphreys, came from a Powys family, was once America's 'most wanted man' and took control of 'the Mob' following the imprisonment of his employer.

In terms of geography Ellis Island, off New York's Manhattan, was established by Samuel Ellis from Wrexham and Roger Williams is responsible for Rhode Island.

Sir Henry Morton Stanley from Denbigh uttered the words "Dr Livingstone I presume" when he 'found' the Scottish missionary and explorer apparently missing in Africa in search of the source of the Nile. He had travelled to the US and after becoming a journalist (indeed as one of the first 'star' reporters) was commissioned by the New York Herald to find the whereabouts of Livingstone.

Tying a yellow ribbon around a tree was originally a Welsh tradition from the 18th century. Way before the homecoming of a Georgia prisoner inspired the 1973 hit 'Tie a Yellow Ribbon Round the Ole Oak Tree' by Dawn featuring Tony Orlando, Welsh settlers in America planted daffodils outside their homes to welcome new arrivals. Later on they used yellow ribbon tied around a tree instead so new immigrants would know where their fellow countrymen were living.

Other Welsh-American Influences

*   Welshman George Jones co-founded The New York Times;

*   American universities Yale, Princeton, Brown, Harvard and Andover were all founded by Welshmen;

*   Hillary Rodham Clinton is of Welsh descent and is said to be immensely proud of this fact;

*   The real Indiana Jones (the 19th century Governor Jones of Indiana) was Welsh;

*   Jack Daniels, the American whisky man, was of Welsh descent - his family came from Aberystwyth.

Australia

*   The 1914 Prime Minister of Australia was Welshman William Hughes;

*   Rolf Harris, Danni and Kylie Minogue's ancestry can be traced back to Merthyr Tydfil.

Welsh Societies Outside Wales

America

Alabama Welsh Society

Cambrian Heritage Society of Madison Wisconsin

Carbondale Welsh Society

Colorado Welsh Society

Cymdeithas Madog - (Welsh Studies Institute of North America, Inc)

Gulf Coast St David's Society

Iowa Welsh Society

Knoxville Welsh Society

New York Welsh/Cymraeg Efrog Newydd

North American Association for the Study of Welsh Culture and History (NAASWCH)

Oklahoma Welsh Society

Poultney Area St David's Society

Puget Sound Welsh Association (PSWA)

Quad Cities Welsh Society

Saint David's Society of Connecticut

Saint David's Society of St Petersburg and the Suncoast

Saint David's Society of Wyoming Valley

Saint David's Welsh-American Society of Baltimore

Saint David's Welsh Society of the Capital District

Saint David's Welsh Society of Georgia

Saint David's Welsh Society of Greater Kansas City

Saint David's Welsh Society of Michigan

Saint David's Welsh Society of Nebraska

Saint David's Welsh Society of the Slate Belt, Bangor, Pennsylvania

St David's Society of Utica, NY

St David's Welsh American Society of Washington, DC

SWSNY

The Chicago Tafia

The Idaho Welsh Society

The St David's Society of Pittsburgh

The Susquehanna Valley Welsh Society

The Welsh American Cultural Organizations of Greater Chicago

Utah Welsh Society

Wales International/Cymru A'r Byd

Welsh-American Genealogical Society (WAGS)

Welsh American Society of Northern California

Welsh League of Arizona

Welsh National Gymanfa Ganu Association

Welsh North American Chamber of Commerce/ Siambr Masnach Cymru-Gogledd America

Welsh Organizations in the Washington, DC Area

Welsh Society of the Carolinas

Welsh Society of Central Ohio

Welsh Society of Fredricksburg

Welsh Society of Greater Cincinnati

Welsh Society of Northwest Ohio/Cymdeithas Gymraeg Gogledd Orllewin Ohio

Welsh Society of Philadelphia/Cymdeithas Gymreig Philadelphia

Welsh Society of Western New England

Women's Welsh Clubs of America/Y Cartref Cymru

Australia

St David's Welsh Society of Brisbane, Inc

Welsh Society of Southern Tasmania

Y Gymdeithas Gymreig Sydney/The Welsh Society of Sydney

Belgium

Brussels Welsh Society

Canada

Prince Edward Island Welsh Society

Saint David's Society of Montreal

Saint David's Society of Toronto

Saint David's Society of Winnipeg/Cymdeithas Dewi Sant Winnipeg

The English/Welsh Society of Saskatoon

The St David's Welsh Society of Edmonton

Victoria Welsh Society

Welsh Association of the Pacific Northwest

Welsh Society of Vancouver

Dubai

Dubai Welsh Society

England

Cymdeithas Cymry Birkenhead

Cymry Llundain

SWS

Finland

The Finnish Welsh Society

France

Paris Welsh Society

Hong Kong

Hong Kong Welsh Society

Japan

St David's Society Japan

New Zealand

Welsh Cambrian Society of Canterbury New
Zealand Inc/Cymdeithas Gymraeg Caergaint
Seland Newydd Cyf

Norway

Oslo Welsh Society/Cymdeithas Cymru Oslo

Festivals & Events

Llangollen International Musical Eisteddfod

Llangollen International Musical Eisteddfod has been held annually since 1947. Over 100,000 visitors from across the world descend on the town during the festival and in 2002 it was declared the UK's first eurozone.

Royal Welsh Show

The Royal Welsh Show in July has a permanent showground at Builth Wells from where farming in Wales is annually exhibited. The Show attracts more than 200,000 visitors over four days, up to 7,000 entries of livestock and over 1,000 trade stands covering the whole of farming life in Wales.

Abergavenny Food Festival

The Abergavenny Food Festival takes place over a September weekend. On the edge of the Brecon Beacons, thousands of food lovers assemble to celebrate the "Greatest Event in Wales" (Wales Tourist Board 2003).

Masterclasses, tutored tastings, walks, talks and demonstrations are offered plus market stalls and lively street entertainment. A huge draw to the festival are the food demonstrations given by professional chefs akin to, for example, Franco Taruschio, former patriarch of the Walnut Tree Inn.

Big Cheese Festival

The 19th century Caerphilly Cheese Race has been revived thanks to this annual summer festival celebrating the crumbly export. This free event, which brings in thousands of visitors to the town, combines historical re-enactments, arts and crafts displays, a funfair and a fireworks display.

Hay Festival

Hay-on-Wye is a tiny market town in the Wye Valley on the edge of the Brecon Beacons National Park. It has a population of 1,300 and 39 bookshops. For ten days in May/June every year 80,000 visitors converge on Hay from all over Europe and America to enjoy the performances of stage, screen and radio stars.

Alongside this is the Children's Festival where workshops in storytelling, puppetry and magic occupy children between the ages of 6-12.

Brecon Jazz Festival

The world famous Brecon Jazz, "a leader in its field", is an annual festival taking place in August each year. Its innovative programme and reputation for attracting top musicians puts it among the best of Europe's jazz festivals.

Vale of Glamorgan Festival

The Vale of Glamorgan Festival was formed in 1969 by John Metcalf, its present Artistic Director. The festival is the most adventurous and unique in the UK for its total concentration on the work of living composers only. Taking place during September, artists of international quality give performances in a variety of venues within the Vale of Glamorgan.

Cardiff Screen Festival

The oldest film festival in Wales originated in Aberystwyth and now invites the world to Cardiff to present the best of Wales over ten days every November.

An unrivalled feature of the festival is the annual presentation of the DM Davies award which is Europe's single largest short film prize. It is proffered to the director who is of Welsh origin, or who has been resident in Wales for two or more years, for the best short film submitted to the competition. Previous winners include Justin Kerrigan for 'Human Traffic' and Sara Sugarman for 'Very Annie Mary'.

World Bog Snorkelling Championships

An annual international sporting event which takes place over the August Bank Holiday. Domestic and international competitors (some as far-flung as

America and Australia) snorkel their way through Waen Rhydd Peat Bog in Llanwrtyd Wells, Powys.

Competitors complete two lengths of a 55 metre trench wearing flippers and snorkel without using any conventional swimming strokes.

The event was cancelled in 2001 because of Foot and Mouth and previously to that no wet suits were required as the bog dried up in an unusually hot summer.

World Mountain Bike Bog Snorkelling Championships

In recent years the World Bog Snorkelling Championships has inspired a similar event replacing flippers with spokes. On the outskirts of Llanwrtyd Wells competitors in the World Mountain Bike Bog Snorkelling Championships cycle two lengths of a bog, around 90 metres, using snorkels and riding specially prepared mountain bikes with the tyres filled with lead and water.

Wales Rally GB

Rugged forestry and the mountains of south, mid and west Wales provide locations for 19 stages of rallying over four days.

PortmeiriCon

'Six of One' (The Prisoner Official Appreciation Society) holds an annual convention in the

Portmeirion Hotel every March. Entertainments include serious debate, enactments, screen presentations, games like 'Human Chess', celebrity guests and a re-creation of the 'Village' where the 17 episodes of 'The Prisoner' were filmed and the fantasy 'No. 6' tried to escape from each time.

Food

"Only the soul can starve to death with food about."
(quoted from Rape of the Fair Country by Alexander
Cordell)

The income from mining and agriculture and large
families dictated, for centuries, a very simple and basic
diet in Welsh kitchens. Ingredients were largely grown,
collected or caught and prepared in a pot and/or on a
bakestone on an open hearth.

A modern staple, origin unknown, is now 'half and
half' (or 'aff 'n' aff' as it is colloquially known) which is,
Atkins dieters exempt, half rice and half chips.

Traditional Recipes

Caws Wedi Pobi (Welsh Rarebit)

Fantastic snack fodder at any time of day. Particularly good for late night munchies or for assistance with a hangover.

4 slices of bread (any kind according to preference or availability, with or without the crusts)

8 ozs (225 g) cheddar cheese

2 ozs (50 g) butter

¼ pint (150 ml) milk

1 tsp mustard

Melt the butter in saucepan, then add the cheese and milk. Stir continuously until soft and smooth. Add the mustard.

Toast the bread. Stir the cheese sauce mixture well. Pour over the toasts and and place under a grill until bubbling and golden brown. Serve at once adding salt and pepper if desired.

Bara Lawr (Laver Bread)

Laver is an edible seaweed commonly found on the south-west coast of Wales. That explains the 'laver' but unfortunately not the 'bread'.

4 ozs (125 g) prepared laver bread

1 oz (25 g) medium/fine oatmeal

1 egg

a little plain flour

bacon fat or butter to fry

Beat the egg, mix with the laver bread and oatmeal. Form into about six balls, roll them in the flour and flatten into little cakes (patties). Fry in the fat, turn over once and serve with bacon and eggs.

Vegetarian Option Laver Bread

1 lb (450 g) prepared laver bread

4 oz (100 g) oatmeal

2 tbsp vegetable oil

Mix together the laver bread and the oatmeal in a large mixing bowl. Form into balls, about 2 inches (5 cm) across and ¾ inch (2 cm) in thickness, and flatten into little cakes (patties). Heat the oil until very hot then fry the cakes for 2 minutes on each side. Drain on kitchen paper and serve immediately.

Cawl (Soup/Broth)

Cawl is a simple stew of available meat (originally mutton) and seasonal vegetables cooked in a large pot. It can be eaten as a meal in itself with bread and cheese but some households like to take the broth as a starter and the meat and vegetables as the main course. The origins and recipe for Lobscows (Lobscouse) are similar and there is evidence to suggest that both are colloquial versions of the same dish - Lobscows in the north and Cawl in the south.

2 lbs (900 g) of ham, shin, mutton or lamb

1 lb (450 g) onions

1 lb (450 g) leeks

1 lb (450 g) carrots

1 small swede, turnip or parsnip

2 lbs (900 g) potatoes

1 tbsp lard or bacon fat (optional)

salt and pepper

sprig of thyme (optional)

water

Remove excess fat from the meat and cut into small pieces. Prepare all the vegetables by peeling and cutting into cubes or small pieces.

In a large saucepan brown the vegetables in the lard or bacon fat, remove, then brown the meat and reunite with the vegetables. Alternatively, simply place the whole lot in the saucepan and cover with water. Add salt and pepper (and the thyme if you are so inclined) and bring to the boil. Simmer for at least 1 ½-2 hours. Taste and add more seasoning if required.

Welsh Cakes

Are they cakes or biscuits? The debate has been running far longer than the 'Jaffa Cakes' one. Both 'Jaffa' and 'Welsh' have cake in their title which suggests that they are, naturally, cakes. However, the 'Welsh' dimensions (circumference, density, overall size, hand to mouth distance) infer that they should be classed as biscuits. In the wider, and more pragmatic spectrum, they are usually on sale in the cake section of supermarkets.

That said; they taste MUCH better home-made, which leaves their literal and eventual outcome entirely dependent on the size of your 'cookie cutter'.

8 oz (200 g) self-raising flour

4 oz (100 g) butter or good quality margarine

2 oz (50 g) granulated sugar and a little caster sugar to serve

2-3 oz (50-75 g) currants (glacé cherries can be used as an alternative for fun although not traditional)

1 egg

2 tbsp milk

Rub the fat and the flour together until crumbly. Add the other ingredients followed by the egg and, carefully, the milk (sticky dough is best avoided).

Roll out to ¼-½ an inch (0.75-1.5 cm) and cut into rounds of between 1 ½-2 inches (3-5 cm) across depending on whether you want the small or standard sized ones.

Traditionally, Welsh Cakes were cooked on a griddle but this recipe also allows for the use of a frying pan. Turn once or twice until brown (usually 3-5 minutes). Dust with a little caster sugar to serve or leave to cool and enjoy with butter and/or jam.

Bara Brith (Speckled Bread)

1 lb (450 g) self-raising flour

1 lb (450 g) mixed dried fruit

½ pint (300 ml) tea

1 egg, beaten

6 tbsp soft brown sugar

2 tbsp marmalade

1 tsp mixed spice

honey to glaze

Soak the fruit overnight in the tea. The following day mix together the marmalade, egg, sugar, spice and flour. Spoon into a greased loaf tin and bake in a warm oven (325°F/170°C) for 1 ¾ hours or until the centre is cooked through. Check from time to time that the top doesn't brown too much - cover with foil or move down a shelf if necessary.

Once cooked, leave to stand for a few minutes. Then tip out on to a cooling tray and glaze the top with honey. Serve sliced with salted butter. My mamgu (grandmother) would facilitate this by holding the bread like a baby once she had cut the end off, buttering from the top and carving slice by thin slice.

Other Foods

Caerphilly Cheese

Caerphilly cheese is a crumbly, moist and creamy white vegetarian cheese traditionally of south and west Wales although it is now mostly made in Somerset. The cheese first sold in the area around the town of Caerphilly in 1830 was produced by the local farms for domestic use in order to use up surplus milk. This gave the Caerphilly Cheese Market its legs due to demand by the miners who would eat it to replace the salt lost down the pits.

Castle Dairies on the Pontygwindy Industrial Estate still produces the cheese despite a 1995 EC attempt to scupper the trade by declaring it illegal to take delivery of unpasteurised milk in metal churns.

The 19th century Caerphilly Cheese Race has recently been revived, thanks to the Big Cheese Festival, involving running a truckle across a bridge and around the castle grounds.

Pot Noodle

Although not a traditional Welsh dish the Pot Noodle deserves a mention as the cheap student staple was born and brought up in Wales. The don of all snacks has been made in Wales since 1979 and currently produces 170 million pots a year from a factory at Crumlin in Gwent to cater for the rate of consumption which is said to be five a second.

Drink

Captain Morgan Rum

Captain Henry Morgan was a 17th century privateer in the Caribbean. Originally from Llanrumney, a Cardiff suburb, he ruled the waves perpetuated by fiction and the well-known brand of rum. Privateers enjoyed the official support of their governments while also profiting, personally, from their adventures.

Sent to break the Spanish stranglehold on the colonies he executed an attack on Portobello, in modern-day Panama, in 1668 retrieving a number of British prisoners from brutal captivity. The episode is commemorated in the name of the famous London street.

Welsh Wine

Global warming has contributed positively to thriving vineyards and a burgeoning industry in Welsh wine.

Producers include:

* Cwm Deri Vineyard, Martletwy, Pembrokeshire;

* Glyndŵr Vineyard, Llanblethian, Cowbridge, Vale of Glamorgan;

* Gwinllan Padig, Caeowen, Cemaes, Anglesey;

* Llanerch Vineyard, Hensol, Pendoylan, Vale of Glamorgan;

* Monnow Valley Vineyard, Great Osbaston Farm, Monmouth;

* Parva Farm Vineyard, Tintern, Chepstow;

* Sugar Loaf Vineyard, Pentre Lane, Abergavenny;

* Wernddu Vineyard, Pen-y-Clawdd, Monmouth;

* Worthenbury Wines, The Old Rectory, Wrexham.

Breweries and Beers

There has been a boom in micro-brewing throughout Wales. This would not have happened without the Campaign for Real Ale (CAMRA). The campaign has branches throughout Wales, actively promoting Welsh beer and a number of beer festivals are held throughout the year including the Great Welsh Beer and Cider Festival held in Cardiff.

Brains, Cardiff

The most prominent Welsh brewery, still in family ownership they merged with Crown Buckley 1997. The brewery in Cardiff is the former Hancocks brewery owned by Bass.

Regular beers: Brains Dark, Brains Best Bitter, Brains SA (locally referred to as 'skull attack'), Rev James, Buckley IPA.

Breconshire, Brecon

Formed in 2002 by a wholesaler and distributor, a number of their beers are also available bottle-conditioned.

Regular beers: Brecon County Ale, Golden Valley, Red Dragon, Ramblers Ruin.

Bryncelyn, Ystalyfera

A small brewery set up in 1999, the owner is a Buddy Holly fanatic and has named beers in his honour.

Regular beers: Holly Hop, Buddy Marvellous, Buddy's Delight, Oh Boy, Rave On, Buddy Confusing.

Bulmastif, Cardiff

One of the first breweries in the new generation of micro-breweries, well known to real enthusiasts throughout Britain.

Regular beers: Welsh Gold, Jack The Lad, Thoroughbred, Welsh Red, Welsh Black, Brindle, Son of a Bitch.

Bragdy Ceredigion, Cardiganshire

They use no chemical additives, brew an organic beer (Flowerface) and their bottle-conditioned beers are vegan.

Regular beers: Ysbryd o'r Goeden/Spirit of the Forest, Gwrach Ddu/Black Witch, Draig Aur/Golden Dragon, Barcud Coch/Red Kite, Blodeuwedd/ Flowerface, Cwrw 2000/Ale 2000, Yr Hen Darw Du/ Old Black Bull.

Coles, Llanddarog

Based at a 14th century pub using its own water supply. They are able to brew in small volumes, enabling them to brew many different beers.

Regular beers: Nettle Ale, Oaten Barley Stout, Black Stag, Roasted Barley Stout, Cwrw Betys (Beetroot Ale), Cwrw Llanddarog, Cwrw Blasus, Dewi Sant.

Conwy, Conwy

Recently formed with assistance from the Welsh Assembly Government.

Regular beers: Castle Bitter, Celebration Ale, Honey Fayre.

Cwmbran, Upper Cwmbran

All their beer is brewed from water drawn from a mountain spring.

Regular beers: Double Hop, Crow Valley Bitter, Crow Valley Stout/Deryn Du, Four Seasons, Full Malty, Gorse Porter.

Felinfoel, Felinfoel

The oldest brewery in Wales, and in the 1930s, became the first brewery in Europe to can beer.

Regular beers: Dragon Bitter Ale, Best Bitter, Double Dragon Ale.

Nags Head, Abercych

A pub brewery that has one beer.

Regular beer: Old Emrys.

Plassey, Wrexham

Founded in 1985 on the Plassey Estate which has three outlets for their beer.

Regular beers: Welsh Border Exhibition Ale, Bitter, Fusilier, Cwrw Tudno, Dragon's Breath.

Snowdonia, Waunfawr

Based in the old stationmaster's house at the terminus of the Welsh Highland Railway. Many one-off beers have been brewed.

Regular beer: Welsh Highland Bitter.

Swansea, Bishopston

Based at the Joiners Arms it supplies a small number of outlets.

Regular beers: Deep Slade Dark, Bishopswood Bitter, Three Cliffs Gold, Original Wood.

Tomas Watkin, Swansea

A fair sized brewery supplying 100 or so pubs.

Regular beers: Watkin's Woosh, Brewery Bitter, Merlin Stout, Old Style Bitter.

Travellers Inn, Caerwys

A brewery that only brews beer when the brewer feels the urge!

Regular beer: Roy Morgan's Original Ale.

Warcop, St Brides Wentlooge

A small brewery that has a portfolio that is too long to list. A number of beers take their names from the area's mining heritage.

Regular beers: Pit Shaft, Pitside, Pit Prop, Drillers, Deep Pit.

Ynys Môn, Talwrn

Facing the mountains of Snowdonia, their cask beers are also available in bottle-conditioned form and suitable for vegans.

Regular beers: Medra, Wennol, Seuruik, Sosban Fach, Tarw Du, Amnesia.

Arts

Arts Practitioners

The inclusion of film and TV references are merely an aid to recognition and not intended to be comprehensive.

Actors

Sir Stanley Baker - *Ferndale*

[Captain Horatio Hornblower R.N./Knights of the Round Table/Richard III/Helen of Troy/ Alexander the Great/Hell Drivers/Blind Date/The Guns of Navarone/Eva/Sodom and Gomorrah/Zulu (which he also produced)/Sands of the Kalahari/ The Italian Job (which he also produced)/Innocent Bystanders/Zorro]

Christian Bale - *Haverfordwest*

[The Machinist/Captain Corelli's Mandolin/ American Psycho/Velvet Goldmine/Empire of the Sun]

Hywel Bennett - *Garnant*

[Best known for playing the TV detective 'Shelley']

Richard Burton - *Pontrhydyfen*

[Nineteen Eighty-Four/The Wild Geese/Equus/ Under Milk Wood/Where Eagles Dare/Who's Afraid of Virginia Woolf?/Hamlet/Zulu/Cleopatra/Look Back in Anger/The Last Days of Dolwyn]

Timothy Dalton - *Colwyn Bay*

[Best known for playing 'James Bond' in Licence to Kill and The Living Daylights]

Meredith Edwards - *Rhosllannerchrugog*

[Film: Going Home/Gulliver's Travels/The Great St Trinian's Train Robbery/Only Two Can Play/ The Trials of Oscar Wilde/Tiger Bay/Dunkirk/The Lavender Hill Mob/A Run for Your Money; TV: The Old Devils/The Life and Times of David Lloyd George/ The Saint]

Clifford Evans - *Senghenydd*

[Film: Valley of Song/Love on the Dole/The Proud Valley; TV: The Prisoner/The Avengers/The Saint/ Randall and Hopkirk (Deceased)]

Hugh Griffith - *Anglesey*

[Film: A Nightingale Sang in Berkeley Square/ The Hound of the Baskervilles/Wuthering Heights/ Oliver!/How to Steal a Million/Tom Jones/Mutiny on the Bounty/Ben Hur/Kind Hearts and Coronets/ The Last Days of Dolwyn/Neutral Port; TV: Grand

Slam/The 33rd Annual Academy Awards (which he presented)/The Citadel]

Kenneth Griffith - *Tenby*

[Film: Very Annie Mary/The Englishman Who Went Up a Hill But Came Down a Mountain/Four Weddings and a Funeral/The Wild Geese/Jane Eyre/The Whisperers/Only Two Can Play/Tiger Bay/A Night to Remember/Blue Murder at St Trinian's/Private's Progress/The Prisoner/High Treason/Blue Scar/The Farmer's Wife/Love on the Dole; TV: Holby City/Lovejoy/Minder/The Prisoner (in an episode which he co-wrote)]

Ioan Gruffudd - *Cardiff*

[Film: King Arthur/Very Annie Mary/102 Dalmatians/Solomon and Gaenor/Titanic/Wilde; TV: Hornblower/Man and Boy/Great Expectations]

Sir Anthony Hopkins - *Margam*

[Meet Joe Black//The Mask of Zorrow/August/Shadowlands/The Remains of the Day/Howards End/The Silence of the Lambs/The Bounty/The Elephant Man]

Donald Houston - *Tonypandy*

[Film: Clash of the Titans/Voyage of the Damned/Sunstruck/Where Eagles Dare/Carry On Jack/Doctor in Distress/Twice Round the Daffodils/Doctor in the House/The Blue Lagoon;

TV: Return of the Saint/Department S/The Prince and the Pauper]

Rhys Ifans - *Ruthin*

[Janice Beard: 45 Words Per Minute/Rancid Aluminium/Kevin & Perry Go Large/The Shipping News/Once Upon a Time in the Midlands/Notting Hill]

Roger Livesey - *Barry*

[Hamlet/The Amorous Adventures of Moll Flanders/The Entertainer/Green Grow the Rushes/ A Matter of Life and Death/The Life and Death of Colonel Blimp/Lorna Doone]

Desmond Llewellyn - *Newport, Gwent*

[Best known for playing 'Q' in 17 Bond movies]

Philip Madoc - *Merthyr Tydfil*

[He Knew He Was Right/A Mind to Kill/The Life and Times of David Lloyd George/Poldark/Porridge/ Dad's Army]

Ray Milland - *Neath*

[Film: Slavers/Aces High/Love Story/Hostile Witness/The Girl in the Red Velvet Swing/Dial M for Murder/Night Into Morning/A Woman of Distinction/It Happens Every Spring/The Trouble with Women/The Lost Weekend (for which he was the first Welsh actor to win an Oscar)/Reap the Wild Wind/The Doctor Takes a Wife/Everything

Happens at Night/Beau Geste/Ebb Tide/The Gilded Lily/Bolero; TV: Hart to Hart/Charlie's Angels/ Love Boat/Fantasy Island/Battlestar Galactica/ Meet Mr McNulty]

Jonathan Pryce - *Holywell*

[Pirates of the Caribbean: The Curse of the Black Pearl/Very Annie Mary/The Testimony of Taliesin Jones/Ronin/Tomorrow Never Dies/Glengarry Glen Ross/The Rachel Papers/The Adventures of Baron Munchausen/Jumpin' Jack Flash/Brazil/ Breaking Glass]

Robert Pugh - *Pontypridd*

[Film: Master and Commander: The Far Side of the World/Plots with a View/Enigma/The Testimony of Taliesin Jones/The Englishman Who Went Up a Hill But Came Down a Mountain; TV: Prime Suspect 6/Clocking Off/The Lakes/A Dance to the Music of Time/Drovers' Gold/Brookside]

Matthew Rhys - *Cardiff*

[Very Annie Mary/The Testimony of Taliesin Jones/House of America]

John Rhys-Davies - *Salisbury, Wiltshire*

[Best known for playing 'Gimli' in The Lord of the Rings trilogy and 'Sallah' in the Indiana Jones trilogy]

Tom Ward - *Swansea*

[Red Cap/Love in a Cold Climate/Anna Karenina/ Midsomer Murders/Silent Witness/Pride and Prejudice]

Actresses

Catherine Zeta Jones - *Mumbles*

[Film: The Terminal/Intolerable Cruelty/Chicago/ America's Sweethearts/Traffic/High Fidelity/ Entrapment/The Mask of Zorro; TV: The Cinder Path/ The Darling Buds of May]

Ruth Madoc - *Norwich, Norfolk*

[Best known for playing 'Gladys Pugh' in Hi-de-hi!]

Siân Phillips - *Betws*

[Film: House of America/Dune/Under Milk Wood/Goodbye, Mr Chips; TV: Attila/Alice Through the Looking Glass/The Chestnut Soldier/Emlyn's Moon/The Snow Spider/Tinker, Tailor, Soldier, Spy/ I, Claudius]

Rachel Roberts - *Llanelli*

[Foul Play/Picnic at Hanging Rock/Murder on the Orient Express/Saturday Night and Sunday Morning/ Our Man in Havana/Valley of Song]

Rachel Thomas - *Alltwen*

[Under Milk Wood/Tiger Bay/Valley of Song/
Blue Scar/The Captive Heart/The/Halfway House/
Undercover/The Proud Valley]

Artists

Nina Hamnett - Tenby

Augustus John - Tenby

Gwen John - Haverfordwest

Thomas Jones - Pencerrig

Andrew Vicari - Port Talbot

Sir Kyffin Williams - Llangefni

Richard Wilson - Montgomeryshire

Comedians

Peter Baynham - *Canton, Cardiff*

[Friday Night Armistice/Knowing Me, Knowing
You with Alan Partridge/The Day Today]

Rob Brydon - *Swansea*

[The Keith Barret Show/Directors Commentary/
Marion and Geoff]

Tommy Cooper - *Caerphilly*

Dawn French - *Holyhead*

[The Vicar of Dibley/French and Saunders/Girls on Top/The Comic Strip Presents]

Designers

Laura Ashley - Merthyr Tydfil

Jeff Banks - Ebbw Vale

David Emmanuel - Bridgend

Julien MacDonald - Merthyr Tydfil

Molly Parkin - Pontycymmer

Entertainers

Max Boyce - Glynneath

Ivor Emmanuel - Pontrhydyfen

Russell Grant - Cardiff

'Two Ton' Tessie O 'Shea - Cardiff

Harry Secombe - Swansea

Victor Spinetti - Ebbw Vale

Poetry & Literature

Wales has inspired writers and poets, both indigenous and visiting, for centuries - Noel Coward, for example, wrote 'Blithe Spirit' at Portmeirion and Lewis Carroll created 'Alice in Wonderland' in Llandudno.

Folklore Tales

The Mabinogion

A masterpiece of medieval literature, The Mabinogion is regarded by many as Wales' greatest contribution to European literature giving rise to the fantasy fiction genre which was practically unknown before its publication.

It first came to general literary prominence in the mid-19th century when Lady Charlotte Guest published her translation of the 11 folk tales under the title of The Mabinogion, a series which originated from around the 11th and 12th centuries although they can be considered much older as they were passed down orally through the generations.

Preserved in written form in the White Book of Rhydderch (1300-1325) and the Red Book of Hergest (1375-1425) the four heroic branches of Pwyll, Branwen, Manawydan, and Math are linked by Pryderi; and the tales themselves are set in a magical landscape which accommodate white horses, giants, beautiful women and heroic men.

Later Folklore Tales

Cantre'r Gwaelod

The duty officer Seithenyn is said to have been drunk in charge of the watchtower one night at Aberdyfi and missed the tidal wave that sank Cantre'r Gwaelod (the hundred towns at the bottom). Borth near Aberystwyth is said to have been the 100th, his carelessness passed into folklore, Merionethshire apparently became teetotal for a decade and the estuary still appears desolate and haunting.

Y Ferch o Gefn Ydfa

'Y Ferch o Gefn Ydfa' (The Maid from Cefn Ydfa) is a tragic early 18th century love story which is distinctive as a legendary tale as it is true. It illustrates the exquisite passion of the Welsh and also gave Wales one of its classic love songs, 'Bugeilio'r Gwenith Gwyn' (Watching The White Wheat), the first verse of which follows:

Mi sydd fachgen ieuanc ffôl

Yn byw yn ôl fy ffansi

Myfi'n bugeilio'r gwenith gwyn

Ac arall yn ei fedi.

Pam na ddeu di ar fy ôl

Ryw ddydd ar ôl ei gilydd?

Gwaith 'rwyn dy weld, y feinir fach

Yn lanach, lanach beunydd!

The song is said to have been written by the male lead, a labourer called Wil Hopcyn from Llangynwyd, Tir Iarll, in Glamorgan in order to distract himself as he had fallen for Ann Thomas, the heiress to the wealthy local estate of Cefn Ydfa.

They became entwined when he was called to work on the roof of the house which Ann's mother didn't like at all as she was hoping for Anthony Maddocks as a son-in-law, a solicitor from Cefn Risca in nearby Tondu.

They both continued to meet in secret until Ann's mother found out and grounded her. Nevertheless her faithful maid maintained communication links by hiding notes in a hollow tree near the house. When the mother discovered this Ann's writing materials were seized. Once again, however, she overcame the difficulty by writing to her lover on sycamore leaves using a needle as a writing implement and her own blood as ink.

The maid was sacked and Ann married Maddocks. However, so heavy was her heart that she began to wither. Hopcyn was summoned to the house but she died in his arms. She was 23. They were buried together and their resting place has become a tourist attraction.

Authors and Poets

The metres and forms used in Welsh poetry are quite different from those in use in English. The 'englyn' (an alliterative stanza) being the most popular in the early period, 'Cynghanedd' (a metrical consonance peculiar to Welsh/a form of assonance) is an important feature of this early poetry and Dafydd ap Gwilym invented and popularised another distinctive metre in the form of the 'cywydd'.

The Middle Ages

Ieuan Fardd (Evan Evans) was a notable scholar who served as a curate in parishes across Wales and England. His determination to promote Welsh cultural assets often brought him into conflict with the Church Of England.

After many years studying ancient manuscripts he published a significant work in 'Some Specimens of the Ancient Welsh Bards'. It contained early Welsh poetry that had previously been unpublished including one of the earliest known works of Welsh literature - *Aneirin's* 6th century epic 'Y Gododdin'.

Gododdin was the geographical area between the Tyne and Forth rivers and the poem, rendered in a variety of metres, remains a classic. It details the extreme bravery of the soldiers of Gododdin who went into battle against the Saxons and the eventual outcome:

"Gwyr a aeth Gatraeth oedd ffraeth eu llu

Glasfedd eu hancwyn - a gwenwyn fu."

Translated by Joseph Clancy as:

"Men went to Catraeth (Catterick) keen their war-band

Pale mead their potion - it was poison."

Taliesin's name is associated with the 'Book of Taliesin' - a collection of poems considered to have been written down in the 10th century but which date from the 6th century. Like Aneirin he was a court poet and some of the poems in the volume are addressed to the kings of the day while the rest of the book concentrates on topics such as mythology and religion.

Throughout the Middle Ages literature continued to thrive and developed because of the patronage of kings and princes of poets and deliberate attempts to permanently record the output. The most famous poet of the period, and generally regarded as the greatest of all time, was *Dafydd ap Gwilym* whose themes included love ('The Girls of Llanbadarn' being one of his vehicles for eyeing-up women) and nature. He has been compared to Chaucer and is regarded as the creator of the metre 'cywydd'.

16th and 17th Centuries

In 1588 *William Morgan*'s translation of the Bible appeared and most of the works published in Welsh for at least the next century were religious in tone.

During this period religion was gaining in importance. By now women were also writing and the seeds of Welsh writing in English began to appear, particularly in the work of *Henry Vaughan* a metaphysical poet and doctor. His love of nature and mysticism was inspired by his native environment around Brecon and has influenced other poets like Wordsworth.

18th Century

The trend in favour of religious literature continued and grew stronger as a result of Nonconformism in Wales. The Methodist Revival, initially led by Howell Harris and Daniel Rowland, produced hymns and poetry by *William Williams Pantycelyn* and others.

As Methodism gathered speed *Ann Griffiths'* short lived (she died aged only 29) but enduring religious poetry and hymns were published. Her 'Casgliad o Hymnau' (Collection of Hymns) was published with a preface by Howell Harris' successor Thomas Charles as his powerful reference text 'Geiriadur Ysgrythurol' (Scriptural Dictionary) was one of the most important influences on her work.

It was around this time that *Iolo Morgannwg* was active in publicising the bardic traditions of Glamorgan including the 'Gorsedd' and *Twm o'r Nant* (Thomas Edwards) was writing poetry and interludes.

19th Century

The Industrial Revolution saw a large influx of people moving into the south Wales valleys and an increase in demand for literature; this is attributed also to the accession of eisteddfods which was evident at the time.

Poets now used bardic names to disguise their identity in competitions, continuing with them when they became well known. The most celebrated of these were William Thomas ('*Islwyn*') and John '*Ceiriog*' Hughes who was, as well as a poet, a well known collector of Welsh folk tunes. His song lyrics include 'Clychau Aberdyfi' (The Bells of Aberdyfi).

The novel had been slow to pick up momentum in Wales but the first recognised novelist in the Welsh language was *Daniel Owen*, author of 'Rhys Lewis' (1885) and 'Enoc Huws' (1891) among others.

The absolutely unconventional *W H Davies* followed, straddling the late 19th and early 20th centuries. He became a writer by accident preventing him from doing any physical work. George Bernard Shaw was stunned by his verse and his itinerant existence in the UK and North America formed the basis of 'The Autobiography of a Super-Tramp' which appeared 25 years before George Orwell's 'Down and Out in Paris and London' and 50 in advance of Jack Kerouac's 'On the Road'.

Among his poems, 'Leisure' is still regarded as a classic, containing the repeatedly quoted:

"What is this life if, full of care,

We have no time to stand and stare?"

20th Century

In the late 19th and early 20th century industrialisation continued to influence, but literature was being utilised as a platform for politicking and in particular the Welsh language was being used as a political symbol. The agricultural way of life which persisted in the countryside however continued to be idealised by many writers.

Poet and scholar *T H Parry-Williams* in 1912 became the first person to win the National Eisteddfod Chair and Crown in the same year and then went on to do the same in 1915. He popularised the sonnet, as did his cousin *R Williams Parry,* and published many papers including 'The English Element in Welsh'.

Hedd Wyn (Ellis Humphrey Evans) was an enthusiastic competitor in the eisteddfods and is widely credited with writing some of the greatest verses of the 20th century.

He was fighting with the Royal Welsh Fusiliers during the First World War and was killed at the Battle of Pilken Ridge in 1917. In September of the same year the National Eisteddfod was staged and Hedd Wyn posthumously declared winner of the Chair for his poem 'Yr Arwr' (The Hero). The Chair was draped in black while the audience looked on in silence and disbelief.

David James Jones was a poet and scholar and also went by the bardic name '*Gwenallt*'. His work on religion and politics was informed by his upbringing in a valley dominated by steelworks which killed his father. This prompted his campaigning against working conditions and his political conscience got him imprisoned at Wormwood Scrubs and Dartmoor during the First World War.

He won the Chair at the 1926 and 1931 National Eisteddfods, published five volumes of poetry containing his experiences of growing up in an industrial community as well as two novels 'Plasau'r Brenin' (The King's Palaces) and 'Ffwrneisiau'

(Furnaces). Plus he was the first editor of the literary journal 'Taliesin'.

Considered Wales' primary poets writing in English and one of the major European poets of the 20th century; *R S Thomas* has been described as the "Solzhenitsyn of Wales", was a contemporary of Dylan Thomas, admired by John Betjeman and a friend of Seamus Heaney who beat him to the Nobel Prize for Literature in 1996.

His work has been described as bleak and angry, his images uncompromising and honest. Landscape, God and the countryside were his great inspirations and he is noted for his nationalism and spirituality.

Dylan Thomas was born in Swansea in 1914 and went on to become an internationally ubiquitous poet (he also wrote short stories and film scripts); equally well known for his hell raising as his verse.

His reputation was made in 1934 with the publication of 'Eighteen Poems', later followed by 'Twenty-five Poems' in 1936, 'Deaths and Entrances' in 1946 and 'Collected Poems' in 1952. In the middle of all this (in 1940) 'Portrait of the Artist as a Young Dog' - his most famous collection of short stories evocative of his home turf saw the light of day. His most famous poem remains 'Fern Hill'.

He wrote 'Do Not Go Gentle Into That Good Night' for his terminally ill father in 1952. Although some say it may have been inspired by his father's increasingly failing eyesight "Do not go gentle into that good night. Rage, rage against the dying of the light." has become one of the most quoted couplets in English verse and the poem features widely at funerals across Wales to this day.

He is remembered primarily for the radio play for voices 'Under Milk Wood' which took ten years to write (first drafted at Newquay) and refined in the family's tin bath surrounded by dolly mixtures placed around the rim.

Bob Dylan took his name from Dylan Thomas as he was such a huge fan.

Poet, dramatist and political activist *Saunders Lewis* co-founded Plaid Cymru in 1925, becoming its president the following year and later lending his support to 'Cymdeithas yr Iaith Gymraeg' (the Welsh Language Society). He used drama to focus attention on his political campaigns, was nominated for the Nobel Prize for Literature in 1970 and by the time of his death had been the most celebrated of living Welsh writers.

The tenacious and compassionate *Rhydwen Williams* won the Crown at the National Eisteddfods of 1946 and 1964. A Rhondda poet and novelist he has depicted the coal-mining society of south Wales, both in its heyday and in its decline, from his own standpoint as a collier's son.

Waldo Williams' language of the hearth was English but his schooling immersed him in Welsh and his poetry, of which there is only one volume, is considered among the classics of the language. 'Y Tangnefeddwyr' (The Peacemakers) spread his gospel as a nationalist and political activist.

He had grown up in an environment that would give him a unique view later in life - he was imprisoned for his political views in the 1940s and 1950s and went freelance when the income tax laws changed allowing him to continue protesting through retaining the government's share of his earnings.

Novelist and publisher *Kate Roberts* is one of the major authors to have written in Welsh. She was born into a slate-mining community in north Wales which conferred on her the ability to write credible characterisations. Described as a master of her craft, some of her work has been translated into other languages including 'Te yn y Grug' (Tea in the Heather) and 'Traed Mewn Cyffion' (Feet in Chains).

Dannie Abse was born into a Jewish family, trained as a doctor and because politics was a feature of the household it galvanised him into wanting to "write political poems". Personal experience is a thread in all his works and his medical experience has given him a highly unusual perspective. 'Ash on a Young Man's Sleeve' is regarded as the best known of his abundant output.

The latter part of the century saw some poets seeking to regain the traditional mastery of verse forms partially to make a political point. *Dic Jones* is one such 'cynghaneddwr' and won the Chair at the National Eisteddfod in 1966 for his skill. He is able to compose verses and/or an 'englyn' in seconds and the impromptu nature of these compositions has developed into a legitimate side show at the National Eisteddfod and a radio institution.

Similarly, the poet and popular performer *Twm Morys* won the Chair at the 2003 National Eisteddfod for his ode on the subject 'Doors'.

Of the modern writers doing their thing in English some stand out particularly for their evocative imagery of a mostly post-industrial Wales. These include *John Evans* whose bleak, negative and alienated style has been compared to authors like William Burroughs; another is *Patrick Jones* whose most famous work is the play 'Everything Must Go' which uses lyrics from the Manic Street Preachers album of the same name, facilitated by the Manic's lyricist and bass player Nicky Wire who is the poet's younger brother.

Other Authors

Roald Dahl - *Llandaff, Cardiff*

[Charlie and the Chocolate Factory/James and the Giant Peach/Tales of the Unexpected]

Ken Follet - *Cardiff*

[The Pillars of the Earth/The Key to Rebecca/The Man from St Petersburg/Lie Down with Lions/Eye of the Needle]

Dick Francis OBE - *Pembrokeshire*

[Come to Grief/Whip Hand/Forfeit/Dead Cert/ The Sport of Queens]

T E Lawrence (Lawrence of Arabia) - *Tremadoc*

[The Seven Pillars of Wisdom]

Leslie Thomas - *Newport, Gwent*

[The Virgin Soldiers]

Music

National Anthem

The Welsh national anthem is one of the oldest anthems in the world. 'Hen Wlad fy Nhadau' (Land of My Fathers) was written by father and son Evan James (lyrics) and James James (tune) in 1856. Unique in anthemic terms, as it mentions the country of origin in the lyrics, a monument to their familial accomplishment is located within Ynysangharad Park in Pontypridd.

Hen Wlad fy Nhadau

mae hen wlad fy nhadau yn annwyl i mi

gwlad beirdd a chantorion, enwogion o fri

ei gwrol ryfelwyr gwladgarwyr tra mad

dros ryddid collasant eu gwaed

cytgan:

gwlad! gwlad! pleidiol wyf i'm gwlad

tra môr yn fur

i'r bur hoff bau

o bydded i'r heniaith barhau

hen Gymru fynyddig, paradwys y bardd

pob dyffryn, pob clogwyn, i'm golwg sydd hardd

trwy deimlad gwladgarol mor swynol yw si

ei nentydd, afonydd i mi

os treisiodd y gelyn fy ngwlad dan ei droed

mae heniaith y Cymry mor fyw ag erioed

ni luddiwyd yr awen gan erchyll law brad

ni thelyn berseiniol fy ngwlad

Translation

A (non-literal) translation is offered merely for clarity and learning as the anthem is always sung in Welsh.

Land of My Fathers

the land of my fathers is dear unto me

old land where the minstrels are honoured and free

its warring defenders so gallant and brave

for freedom their life's blood they gave

chorus:

home! home! true am I to home

while seas secure the land so pure

o may the old language endure

old land of the mountains, the Eden of bards

each gorge and each valley a loveliness guards

through love of my country, charmed voices will be

its streams, and its rivers, to me

though foemen have trampled my land 'neath their feet

the language of Cambria still knows no retreat

the muse is not vanquished by traitor's fell hand

nor silenced the harp of my land

Other Songs

Describing pre-Methodist Wales as a "valley of dry bones" the hymn writer William Williams Pantycelyn was sufficiently moved to write 'Guide Me - O Thou Great Redeemer', an unofficial national song now roared out at rugby matches. It was sung at the opening of the Millennium Stadium in 1999. The tune was written by John Hughes in 1907 and is known as 'Cwm Rhondda' and the English translation is the work of Peter Williams:

Guide me - O Thou great Redeemer -

Pilgrim - through this barren land;

I am weak - but Thou art mighty;

Hold me with Thy powerful hand.

Bread of heaven - bread of heaven -

Feed me till I want no more;

Feed me till I want no more.

Music

Colliery bands and male voice choirs have long since perpetuated the images of Wales and the emotions of the Welsh through song. Increasingly this task has also fallen to rugby fans who dapple their public performances with the chant "Ogi Ogi Ogi" and the reply "Oi Oi Oi".

The following songs should always be filed under 'Popular: Welsh':

Ar Hyd y Nos

Ar Lan y Môr

Bread of Heaven

Calon Lân

Delilah

Hymns and Arias

Men of Harlech

Sosban Fach

We'll Keep a Welcome

Cool Cymru

Wales has forever been known as the Land of Song ('Gwlad y Gân'): traditional harp melodies and folk songs, 'Cerdd Dant' (poetry recitation to instrumental accompaniment) and male voice choirs. The 20th century music scene was more popular in character comprising the likes of Tom Jones, Shirley Bassey, Bonnie Tyler, Shakin' Stevens and The Alarm but bands like the Manic Street Preachers, Catatonia, Stereophonics, Super Furry Animals, Gorky's Zygotic Mynci and the 60ft Dolls have done more to promote Wales than any advertising campaign. The Welsh response to Britpop's Cool Britannia of the mid-1990s devolved into 'Cool Cymru' (Cool Wales) putting the country on the world map of contemporary and popular culture.

World-Class

Naturally, Wales is home to the oldest record shop in the world. Established in 1894, the claim is made by Spillers Records on The Hayes in Cardiff.

Musical Influence Outside Wales

The Velvet Underground

John Cale, from Garnant, met Lou Reed via a Boston University scholarship. Together they formed The Velvet Underground and found themselves at the seat of Andy Warhol's Factory in New York during the mid-1960s.

John Cale's work as a producer (e.g. The Stooges) in the early 1970s directly inspired the punk rock revolution and his music has influenced the way bands like Catatonia and Gorky's Zygotic Mynci write their own.

Very few rock musicians can handle a viola with mandolin strings but his expertise qualified him to write the edgy score for the film 'American Psycho'.

The Velvet Revolution

In the space of a few weeks in November 1989 Czechoslovakia was brought to its knees. Massive protests on the streets of Prague forced the resignation of the Communist Party leadership in what became known as 'the velvet revolution'.

The man of the hour, Vaclav Havel, is said to have been heavily influenced by The Velvet Underground. The playwright was one of the leaders of the dissident Charter 77 movement, spending time in prison for his beliefs. After the collapse of the Communists, he was unanimously elected President of Czechoslovakia.

Owen Morris

Producer, Mastering, Mixing, Production Concept - these are Owen Morris' music credentials. A highly sought after producer, he is responsible for Oasis' 'Definitely Maybe' album and has worked with the likes of U2 and The Verve.

Our Manics in Havana

A handful of years ago the Manic Street Preachers became the first major non-Communist rock act to play the Karl Marx Theatre in Havana since 1979. Among the oldsmobiles of Cuba they found themselves facilitating the nationalist zeal for 'Baby Elian', the Cuban boy who became caught between the US and Cuban governments.

Composers

Harry Parr Davies - Neath

Alun Hoddinott - Bargoed

Ivor Novello - Cardiff

Musicians

Phil Campbell (Motorhead) - Treforest

The Edge (U2) - Llanelli

Brian Hibbard (The Flying Pickets) - Neath

Mike Peters (The Alarm) - Prestatyn

Singers (Classical)

Stuart Burrows - Cilfynydd

Charlotte Church - Cardiff

Bruce Dargavel - Neath

Sir Geraint Evans - Cilfynydd

Rebecca Evans - Pontrhydyfen

Katherine Jenkins - Neath

Aled Jones -Bangor

Della Jones - Neath

Dame Gwyneth Jones - Pontnewydd

Dennis O'Neill - Pontarddulais

Dame Margaret Price - Blackwood

Bryn Terfel - Pantglas

Singers (Popular)

Shirley Bassey - Tiger Bay, Cardiff

Julian Cope (The Teardrop Explodes) - Deri

Andy Fairweather-Low (Amen Corner) - Cardiff

Mary Hopkin - Pontardawe

Tom Jones - Treforest

Cerys Matthews (Catatonia) - Cardiff

Dorothy Squires - Pontyberem

Shakin' Stevens - Ely, Cardiff

Bonnie Tyler - Skewen

Iris Williams - south Wales

Film/ Cinematography, TV & Animation

Wales' Filmic Milestones

* 1896 - the first moving pictures of the Prince of Wales (later King Edward VII) were shot in Cardiff.

* 1913 - Hollywood discovers Wales by filming 'Ivanhoe' at Chepstow Castle employing 500 locals as extra.

* 1932 - first film made in Hollywood but entirely set in Wales ,'The Old Dark House'.

* 1939 - filming begins on 'Proud Valley' starring Paul Robeson, the first British film to feature a black working class hero as lead.

* 1941 - 20th Century Fox's 'How Green Was My Valley' wins five Oscars.

Filmed in Wales

It is widely known that 'The Prisoner' was filmed in Portmeirion but other TV crews have also made 'Doctor Who: The Five Doctors', 'The Lion, the Witch, & the Wardrobe', 'Brideshead Revisited' and 'Streetlife' in the land of indigenous song but indigent production subsidies.

Money aside; the locations offered by the Welsh landscape, skilled production technicians, robust facilities industry and the work of the marketing agencies have seduced film makers into employing Wales as a viable production base. For example, 'Under Milk Wood' and 'Moby Dick' were shot around the harbour in Fishguard, 'Lawrence of Arabia' was filmed in the Merthyr Mawr sand dunes near Bridgend, Meg Ryan starred in 'Restoration' - the period backdrop being offered by Caerphilly Castle, the true story of 'The Englishman Who Went Up a Hill But Came Down a Mountain' was built around Llanrhaeadr-ym-Mochnant, Snowdonia was used to film 'From Russia with Love' and 'First Knight' (more than 30 years apart) and 'Only Two Can Play' (the first X-rated film set in Wales) was filmed in Swansea, Llanelli, Neath and Briton Ferry.

Feature films made (or part made) in Wales include:

<u>1910s</u>

Ivanhoe (1913)

<u>1920s</u>

The Farmer's Wife (1928)

<u>1930s</u>

The Citadel (1938)

1940s

Nine Men (1943)

Undercover (1943)

Blue Scar (1949)

The Last Days of Dolwyn (1949) [Richard Burton's screen debut]

1950s

The Constant Husband (1954)

The Dam Busters (1954)

Moby Dick (1956)

Inn of the Sixth Happiness (1958)

Tiger Bay (1959)

1960s

The Green Helmet (1961)

Lawrence of Arabia (1962)

Only Two Can Play (1962) [the first X-rated film set in Wales]

From Russia with Love (1963)

Carry On Up the Khyber (1968)

1970s

The Tragedy of Macbeth (1971)

Gawain and the Green Knight (1973)

Holiday on the Buses (1973)

Under Milk Wood (1973)

Ghost Story (1974)

Jabberwocky (1977)

1980s

The Falls (1980)

An American Werewolf in London (1981)

Dragonslayer (1981)

Time Bandits (1981)

Owain, Prince of Wales (1983)

Sword of the Valiant (1983)

The Keep (1983)

Milwr Bychan (Boy Soldier)* (1986)

Rhosyn a Rhith (Coming Up Roses)* (1986)

Going Home (1987)

On the Black Hill (1987)

Willow (1988)

1990s

Under Suspicion (1991)

Un Nos Ola Leuad (One Full Moon) (1991)

Hedd Wyn (1992) [first Welsh language film to be nominated for a Best Foreign Language Film Oscar]

Rebecca's Daughters (1992) [holds the record for the longest hiatus between the writing of the screenplay (in 1948 by Dylan Thomas) and the film's release - 44 years]

Princess Caraboo (1994)

Second Best (1994)

The Steal (1994)

First Knight (1995)

Gold Diggers: The Secret of Bear Mountain (1995)

Madagascar Skin (1995)

Restoration (1995)

The Englishman Who Went Up a Hill But Came Down a Mountain (1995)

Y Mapiwr (The Making of Maps) (1995)

August (1996)

Intimate Relations (1996)

Darklands (1997)

House of America (1997)

Mortal Kombat: Annihilation (1997)

The Proposition (1997)

Twin Town (1997)

The Theory of Flight (1998)

Up 'n' Under (1998)

Human Traffic (1999)

Solomon and Gaenor (1999)

<u>2000s</u>

House! (2000)

The Testimony of Taliesin Jones (2000)

Very Annie Mary (2001)

Alone (2002)

Plots with a View (2002)

I Capture the Castle (2003)

I'll Be There (2003)

Lara Croft Tomb Raider: The Cradle of Life (2003)

*Became the first Welsh feature films to play simultaneously in the West End.

The only UK feature film ever made on a contemporary home statesman was a biography of David Lloyd George made in 1918. However, it was thought that an "embarrassing world scandal" would emerge following skulduggery by the magazine 'John Bull' which would effectively scupper its release. The silent biopic 'The Life Story of David Lloyd George' had disappeared completely until it was rediscovered by the National Screen and Sound Archive of Wales in 1994. Found amongst material deposited at the Archive by Viscount Tenby (Lloyd George's grandson) it was fully restored and brought to the screen in 1996.

Allen Raine (Anne Adaliza Puddicombe) was a best selling author from west Wales. Her novel 'A Welsh Singer' featured the first American film contract star Florence Turner and became the most popular film ever issued by Butcher's distribution company in the UK. It also marked the screen debut of Edith Evans.

Film Directors

Marc Evans

(Trauma/My Little Eye/Resurrection Man/House of America) - Cardiff

Peter Greenaway

(The Pillow Book/The Cook the Thief His Wife & Her Lover) - Newport, Gwent

Justin Kerrigan

(Human Traffic) - Cardiff

Sara Sugarman

(Very Annie Mary/Mad Cows) - Rhyl

Journalists/Broadcasters

Dr John Davies

(Historian) - Rhondda

Huw Edwards

(BBC Ten O'Clock News Anchor) - Llanelli

Stephen Evans

(BBC North America Business Correspondent) - Cardiff

Guto Harri

(BBC News 24 Chief Political Correspondent) - Cardiff

Ian Hislop

(Editor Private Eye) - Mumbles, Swansea

John Humphrys

(Radio 4's Today programme) - Cardiff

Peter Stead

(Historian) - Swansea

Wynford Vaughan Thomas

(Historian) - Swansea

Gwyn Alf Williams

(Historian) - Dowlais

TV Presenters

Annabel Giles - Griffithstown

Gareth 'Gaz Top' Jones - St Asaph

Siân Lloyd (ITV Weather) - Maesteg

Helen Willetts (BBC Weather) - Colwyn Bay

Paula Yates - Rhyl

TV Writers

Russell T Davies - *Swansea*

[Linda Green/Queer as Folk/Touching Evil/ Children's Ward/Doctor Who]

Elwyn Jones - *Cwmaman*

[Z Cars/Softly Softly/Dixon of Dock Green]

Terry Jones - *Colwyn Bay*

[Monty Python]

Terry Nation - *Cardiff*

[Blake's 7/Dr Who/The Saint/The Persuaders!/ The Avengers/The Goon Show]

Animation

"Animation has reached more screens in more countries than any other product of Wales' media industries." (Tim Robins and Chris Webster writing in 'Wales on Screen' edited by Steve Blandford). As an industry it has been on a steady incline since the 1980s and continues as a multi-award winning entity.

Greatest hits so far include:

Aaargh Animation's 'Gogs'.

Candy Guard's 'Alternative Fringe', 'Fantastic Person', 'Fatty Issues' and 'Pond Life'.

Joanna Quinn's 'Girls' Night Out', 'Body Beautiful', 'Britannia' and 'Famous Fred' (which was nominated for a Short Film Oscar).

Phil Mulloy's 'Cowboys', 'Sound of Music' and 'Thou Shalt Not Kill'.

S4C's Operavox and Animation Classics strands which commissioned 'Shakespeare - The Animated Tales'.

Siriol's 'SuperTed', 'The Princess and the Goblin' (the first Welsh animation feature co-production) and 'Under Milk Wood' (the first all-Welsh animated feature).

Ivor the Engine and Postman Pat, although inspired by Wales are produced elsewhere.

Sport

Wales has a history of developing world-class sports men and women, being passionate about rugby and building universally recognised sporting arenas. It is also the originator of Lawn Tennis thanks to a Major from north Wales.

Lawn Tennis

The 19th century imaginative adaptation of an old Welsh game, which had it roots in Cerrig y Drudion centuries earlier, became known as Lawn Tennis courtesy of Major Walter Wingfield of Nant Clwyd. The manicured lawns of his home and the publishing of a book of rules encouraged him to patent the game. It increased in popularity following the development of a rubber ball covered with flannel, while its simple rules and grace made it relatively accessible to all social classes.

State of Play

Illustrating the range of sporting achievement in Wales past and present:

BBC Wales' Sports Personality of the Year Past Winners

<u>1950s</u>

Ken Jones

John Disley

Joe Erskine

Dai Rees

Howard Winstone

Graham Moore

1960s

Brian Curvis

Bryn Meredith

Ivor Allchurch

Howard Winstone

Lynn Davies (1964 & 1966)

Clive Rowlands

Howard Winstone

Martyn Woodroffe

Tony Lewis

1970s

David Broome

John Dawes/Wales Rugby Team/Welsh Lions

Richard Meade

Berwyn Price

Gareth Edwards

Arfon Griffiths

Mervyn Davies and the Wales Grand Slam Team

Phil Bennett

Johnny Owen

Terry Griffiths

1980s

Duncan Evans

John Toshack

Steve Barry

Colin Jones

Ian Rush

Steve Jones

Kirsty Wade

Ian Woosnam

Colin Jackson

Stephen Dodd

1990s

Ian Woosnam (1990 & 1991)

Tanni Grey

Colin Jackson (1993 & 1999)

Steve Robinson

Neville Southall

Ryan Giggs

Scott Gibbs

Iwan Thomas

2000s

Tanni Grey-Thompson

Joe Calzaghe

Mark Hughes

Nicole Cooke

BBC Wales' Sports Personality of the Year League Table for 2004

David Davies - Swimming

Nicole Cooke - Cycling

Simon Jones - Cricket

Gareth Thomas - Rugby

Joe Calzaghe - Boxing

Robert Earnshaw - Football

Robert Howley - Rugby

Tim Benjamin - Athletics

Enzo Maccarinelli - Boxing

Kelly Morgan - Badminton

Gareth Jenkins - Rugby

Geraint Jones - Cricket

Shane Williams - Rugby

Hayley Tullett - Athletics

Ryan Giggs - Football

Michaela Breeze - Weightlifting

Phil Mills - Motorsports

Catherine Murphy - Athletics

Christian Malcolm - Athletics

Jayne Ludlow - Football

David Roberts - Swimming

Craig Bellamy - Football

Richard Vaughan - Badminton

Robert Weale - Bowls

Matt Elias - Athletics

Rhiannon Henry - Swimming

Robert Croft - Cricket

Becky Morgan - Golf

Tracy Morris - Athletics

Tom James - Rowing

Cricket

The present Glamorgan CCC was formed in 1888 and since 1921 have been Wales` sole representative in the English County Championship – won in 1948, 1969 and 1997. Glamorgan have also beaten all of the major Test playing nations including Australia who they defeated in successive tours in 1964 and 1968.

In addition, Glamorgan won the one day National League in 1993 and 2002, as well as reaching the Lord's final of the Gillette Cup in 1977 and the Benson and Hedges competition in 2000.

Glamorgan CCC Player of the Year

<u>1977 onwards</u>

Alan Jones

Peter Swart

Tony Cordle

<u>1980s</u>

Javed Miandad (1980 & 1981)

Arthur Francis

Rodney Ontong (1983& 1985)

Alan Lewis Jones

Rodney Ontong

Hugh Morris

Steve Watkin

<u>1990s</u>

Hugh Morris and Alan Butcher

Colin Metson

Hugh Morris

Steve Watkin

Tony Cottey

Steve James (1995 & 1997)

Robert Croft

Darren Thomas

Mike Powell

2000s

A Dale (2000 & 2001)

M P Maynard

Robert Croft and Mike Kasprowicz

Athletes

Jamie Baulch - *Nottingham*

Olympic, World, European and Commonwealth 400 m runner.

Lynn Davies - *Nantymoel*

Greatest achievement was winning Gold at the Tokyo Olympics in 1964 and being the first British athlete to do so at the long jump.

Sport

Colin Jackson MBE - *Cardiff*

One of the greatest athletes in the history of British and Welsh athletics, Colin Jackson is an Olympic and Commonwealth Gold medallist and record breaking hurdler.

Christian Malcolm - *Cardiff*

Olympic and World Championship sprinter and a Commonwealth Silver medallist at 200 m.

Catherine Murphy - *Sheffield*

Catherine Murphy set a new Welsh indoor record of 52.72 seconds on her indoor debut at 400 m in 2001 and became the first woman to win both the 200 m and 400 m at the AAA Indoor Championships. She also competed in the World Indoor Championships of 2001.

Iwan Thomas - *Farnborough*

European, Commonwealth and World Cup champion 400 m runner.

Tanni Grey-Thompson - *Penarth*

Paralympian Gold medallist at 100 m, 200 m, 400 m and 800 m

Hayley Tullett - *Swansea*

Olympic and Commonwealth 1,500 m runner.

Boxers

Jim Driscol - *Cardiff*

'Peerless' Jim Driscol was a world-class Featherweight boxer born in 1880.

Jimmy Wilde - *Tylorstown*

The smallest and lightest World Flyweight champion ever was tagged the 'Mighty Atom' and the 'Tylorstown Terror' and the only boxer from the UK to be accepted in America as the finest in his division. As a boy he worked underground at the local pits and learned his trade at fairground boxing booths. He once stated that his toughest fight had been with his wife Elizabeth over a gambling debt.

Johnny Owen - *Merthyr Tydfil*

Known as the 'Matchstick Man' Johnny Owen's professional career spanned 28 contests with 25 victories, one draw and two defeats. His final and ultimate fight was contesting the WBC World Bantamweight title in 1980.

Joe Calzaghe - *Newbridge*

'The Terminator' won the British Super Middleweight title in his 14th professional fight. He made nine defences before meeting Chris Eubank in 1997 to take the WBO title which he defended a further 14 times.

Darts

Leighton Rees from Pontypridd was the first ever winner of the Embassy World Darts crown in 1978, beating John Lowe to take the inaugural title. A further 17 years would pass before fellow Welshman Ritchie Burnett would win the same title at the Lakeside in 1995.

Football

The Football Association of Wales is the third oldest association in the world, having come into existence in 1876. The Association has governed football in Wales continually since; is a member of FIFA and UEFA and is one of the five associations that make up the International Football Association Board, guardians of the "Laws of the Game".

The National League

At the top of the system is the recently renamed 'Welsh Premier', formerly known as the League of Wales. This is now Wales' national league and the only national competition - all leagues below it operate on a regional basis.

Dream Team

The readers of the 'Wales on Sunday' newspaper, via a voting system, compiled the nation's Dream Team of Welsh all-stars of the century which came out as:

Ivor Allchurch

John Charles

Ryan Giggs

Mark Hughes

Cliff Jones

Joey Jones

Roy Paul

Kevin Ratcliffe

Ian Rush

Alf Sherwood

Neville Southall

Subs: Mike England, Trevor Ford, Jack Kelsey, John Toshack, Terry Yorath

Rugby

"There is a vibrancy and confidence about Wales that I can never remember. Of course there are black spots. Rugby is one. The less said about that the better." (John Humphrys)

Rugby Union

Rugby Union is the national sport of Wales, the Welsh Rugby Union (WRU) having been formed after a meeting of clubs in Neath in March 1881. The team of 15 players wear red jerseys with the Prince of Wales Feathers on and (traditionally) white shorts. They compete annually in the Six Nations Championship, which they have won 22 times outright, and their best result in the World Cup so far is 3rd in 1987.

It has been elevated to form part of the culture, the heart of the nation, and it is said that the real passion in British rugby comes from the Welsh which they love with intensity primarily, maybe, because it has no social boundaries.

Top Ten Caps

Neil Jenkins

Gareth Llewellyn

Ieuan Evans

Gareth Thomas

Robert Howley

Garin Jenkins

Colin Charvis

JPR Williams

Robert Jones

Gareth Edwards

Scott Gibbs

Top Ten Point Scorers

Neil Jenkins*

Paul Thorburn

Stephen Jones

Arwel Thomas

Phil Bennett

Ieuan Evans

Steve Fenwick

Gareth Thomas

Barry John

Jack Bancroft

Gareth Edwards

* Neil Jenkins' junior school headmistress was once so vexed with disciplining him for fighting in the playground that she screeched at him one day, as only a Valleys woman can, "Neil Jenkins! If you want to kick anything go kick a ball." So he went on to become Wales' most capped rugby player and the world record holder for points scored in internationals (1,049).

Snooker

Ray Reardon

Past Master Ray Reardon was born in Tredegar in 1932 and ranked 1st in 1976/7, 1980/81 and 1982/3. His highest break was 147 and the brilliant potter, nicknamed snooker's 'Dracula', was one of snooker's all-time greats. He was the first world number one when the rankings were introduced in 1976 and World Professional Snooker champion six times between 1970 and 1978.

Terry Griffiths

Past Master Terry Griffiths was born in Llanelli in 1947 and ranked 3rd in 1981/82. His highest break was 139 and his deliberate and measured style won him his second ever professional event - the World Professional championship in 1979.

Doug Mountjoy

Past Master Doug Mountjoy, from Tir-y-Berth, was born in 1942 and ranked 5th in 1990/91. 'Bursting' onto the snooker scene winning his very first event, the prestigious Benson & Hedges Masters in 1977, as a professional. He was UK champion in 1978 and 1988.

Matthew Stevens

Professional snooker player Matthew Stevens was born in Carmarthen in 1977 and ranked 6th in 1999/00. His highest break is 147 and, as well as being the Benson & Hedges Masters champion in 2000, he won the Travis Perkins UK championship, against former world champion Stephen Hendry, in 2003.

Mark Williams

Professional snooker player Mark Williams was born in Cwm in 1975 and ranked 1st in 2000/01 to 2001/02 and 2003/04. His highest break is 144 and is regarded by many as the best single ball potter in the game today. The Benson & Hedges championship was his first professional title and he was the first left-handed World Professional champion in 2000 and 2003.

Science

Academics

Prof Clive Granger - *Swansea*

Shares the 2003 Nobel Prize for Economics.

Ernest Jones - *Gowerton*

The psychiatrist who has brought 'analysis', 'shrink' and 'rationalisation' into modern parlance. He organised the world's first psychiatric conference at Salzburg in conjunction with Carl Gustav Jung. He learned German in order to gain a better understanding of Sigmund Freud's ideas, assisted his relocation to England from Vienna and became his official biographer.

Prof Steve Jones - *Aberystwyth*

Makes science, especially genetics and evolution, accessible. Professor of Genetics, author of books on evolution and recipient of the Royal Society's Faraday Medal in 1996 for advancing public understanding of science.

Prof Brian Josephson - *Cardiff*

A Nobel Prize winner, he discovered how an electrical current could flow between two superconductors (materials with zero electrical resistance) even when an insulator was placed between them - this became known as the 'Josephson Effect' entering the dictionary.

Timothy Richard Lewis - *Llangain*

Made important discoveries relating to tropical diseases including elephantiasis and river blindness.

Bertrand Russell - *Trellech*

Philosopher, mathematician, essayist and social critic. Won the Nobel Prize for Literature in 1950. Was the 'Russell' of the Russell – Einstein manifesto.

Alfred Russell Wallace - *Usk*

As a scientist his most important work was conceived while suffering from Malaria in Indonesia. He developed the theory of Natural Selection or "survival of the fittest" at the same time as Charles Darwin whom he presented his findings in a letter to.

Extracts from the work of both were presented in a paper to the Linnean society in 1858 and in the race to the line Darwin's 'On the Origin of Species' accepted the credit.

Inventors

Wendy Boston - *Abergavenny*

In 1954, Welsh toy maker Wendy Boston produced the first truly washable teddy bear.

William Grove - *Swansea*

Inventor of a fuel cell in use by NASA to power onboard communication systems on its Apollo and Shuttle programmes. His earlier battery technology was used to power many American telegraph stations.

David Edward Hughes - *Bala*

Invented a telegraph printer (the Hughes Printer - patented in 1855) and a carbon microphone, the prototype of all microphones in use today.

William Henry Preece - *Caernarvon*

In May 1897 Guglielmo Marconi successfully sent a radio signal from Lavernock Point (off Penarth) to the island of Flat Holm (in the Bristol Channel) proving that radio could operate over water.

WH Preece had decided as a child that sound waves must travel the same way through air as over water via his observations of sound blasting in the slate quarries of Snowdonia. Further down the line as Chief Engineer of the GPO - and later still as a private consultant - he was a key figure in several major advances in communications and perfectly placed to assist Marconi in his efforts. With his backing, Marconi sent the first signals across the Atlantic in 1901 - from Cornwall to Newfoundland.

Robert Recorde - *Tenby*

Inventor of the equals sign '=', the first to write mathematical textbooks in English and thereby introducing Algebra to English speakers (yeah - thanks for that).

Isaac Roberts - *Groes*

Produced the first detailed pictures of the Andromeda nebula, more than two million light years from earth, via a telescope/camera. The 'Roberts' crater on the moon is named after him.

Campaigners & Social Reformers

Wales earliest rebel, Owain Glyndŵr, deeply and profoundly affected the Welsh and still resonates wherever injustice resides.

The Campaigners

Ann Pettit - *Cardiff*

Initiated the march from Cardiff to Greenham Common in 1981 which later grew into the Greenham Common Peace Camp. "All we asked for was a debate with our government about the siting of USA Cruise nuclear missiles in our country. This was refused so we stayed."

Ann and many of the Greenham women continue to campaign. In 2003 they joined the Gloucestershire Weapons Inspectors (GWI) for a mass citizens weapons inspection at USAF Fairford in the Cotswolds.

Dafydd Iwan - *Brynaman*

Chairman of the Welsh Language Society between 1968-1971, Dafydd Iwan has always campaigned for Wales and its language. As a singer/songwriter he has a powerful platform from which to enforce his message of opposition to inequality and oppression all over the world, establishing the Sain record company which become Wales' biggest record label along the way. He also formalised his political stance by becoming a county councillor and President of Plaid Cymru.

David Davies - *Llandinam*

A major player in the construction of the Newtown to Aberystwyth railway, he later developed mines in the Rhondda. Success found 'Davies the Ocean' of The Ocean Coal Company taking on the Bute family cartel, who controlled Cardiff docks, and deciding to build his own at Barry instead.

Dic Penderyn - *Aberavon*

19th century Merthyr Tydfil was the largest town in Wales and because of the ironmasters' treatment of the workers and general political unrest the place was ripe for rebellion. Along with the Newport Rising it was one of the most serious violent outbreaks witnessed on mainland Britain. It is also claimed to be the first time that a red flag was waved as a banner of workers' power.

In the aftermath, Richard Lewis (Dic Penderyn) was singled out as the main protagonist and sentenced to death - a martyr was 'born'.

Elizabeth Andrews - *Rhondda*

Suffragette whose legacy includes the inception of pit-head baths at collieries and the opening of the first nursery school in Wales.

Campaigners & Social Reformers

Elizabeth Phillips Hughes - *Carmarthenshire*

Founded the UK's first teacher training college for women which, by 1984, had become Hughes Hall - a fully recognised college of Cambridge University. 'Bessie' Hughes was the first woman ever to achieve first class honours at degree level and campaigned for universal secondary education.

John Frost - *Newport , Gwent*

A tailor who became a prominent member of The Chartists, campaigning for basic democratic rights. Sacked as a magistrate in 1839, he soon found himself at the head of 3,000 men during the Newport Rising. Escaping the death penalty by being transported to Australia instead, he returned to the UK to see most of the Chartist reforms enshrined in law.

Margaret Haig Thomas - *Rhondda*

Suffragette whose work was instrumental in reforming the Women's Royal Air Force.

OM Edwards and Sir Ifan ab Owen Edwards - *Llanuwchllyn*

Father and son who were pioneers in education. OM birthed 'Cymru'r Plant' (Children's Wales) magazine and Sir Ifan ab Owen Edwards became Wales' first inspector of schools.

Sir Ifan ab Owen Edwards went on to create 'Urdd Gobaith Cymru' (the League of Youth in Wales) during the 1930s and camps at Glan-Llyn (on the shores of

Bala Lake) and at Llangrannog (on the Cardiganshire coast). The Urdd National Eisteddfod matured out of these institutions and the 'Urdd' is responsible for broadcasting the Goodwill Message worldwide every May.

Robert Owen - *Newtown*

A mill owner who changed working conditions for his employees during the Industrial Revolution; laying the foundations for the co-operative movement and the concept of trade unions with his efforts to rid abuse of child labour and introduce profit-sharing.

Simon Weston - *Nelson*

A Falklands hero, Simon Weston was seriously injured aboard the Sir Galahad and found himself at the centre of the most disastrous episode of the war.

Despite enduring burns to half his body he has never been unduly interested in apportioning blame. Instead, the fame and support garnered during his rehabilitation inspired him to set up The Weston Spirit in 1988 - a national charity which continues to help thousands of underprivileged youngsters every year.

Saunders Lewis - *Cheshire*

Alongside his literary output Saunders Lewis had a profound influence on 20th century Welsh politics. A founder of Plaid Cymru, he mounted the 'Bombing School' incident and inspired the creation of 'Cymdeithas Yr Iaith Gymraeg' (the Welsh Language Society) which went on to campaign for the establishment of S4C ('Sianel Pedwar Cymru' - the Welsh fourth television channel).

The Campaigns

Merched Beca (Rebecca's Daughters)

The first example of occupational cross-dressing occurred over the 19th century uprising of the tenant farmers and drovers so enraged by the rent and tolls forced upon them that they set fire to toll-gates and smoked out the householders who managed them. They dressed as women and all took the name Beca (Rebecca) to avoid early detection, the fracas becoming known as the Rebecca Riots. The film of Rebecca's Daughters, released in 1992, was given a '15' certificate in the UK for the cross-dressing alone.

Ysgol Fomio (Bombing School)

In the mid-1930s the Plaid Genedlaethol Cymru (the National Party of Wales) channelled its resources into opposing a scheme by Baldwin's Government to train pilots in effective airborne bombing techniques at Lleyn in north Wales. It was effectively a 'pilot scheme' (sic) to test the validity of the process with a view to setting up other bombing schools in Northumberland and Dorset.

Despite protests, the plan to build the school went ahead in Penyberth near Pwllheli (where the Party was established in 1925). On 8 September 1936 the first example of direct action in the name of Welsh national interest in modern times was carried out by Saunders Lewis, D J Williams and Lewis Valentine. The three were sentenced to nine months in jail at the Old Bailey for arson after the jury in Caernarvon failed to agree on a verdict.

Tryweryn

Tryweryn was the reluctant scene of a hugely controversial plan by Liverpool City Council to drown the valley, and living community, to create a reservoir for its consumers.

17th and 18th century Quakers had already departed for Pennsylvania fleeing persecution. Fast forward to 1945 and Plaid Cymru Party President Gwynfor Evans was strenuously against providing any welcome in this hillside near Bala for the scheme. He formed the Tryweryn Defence Committee to resist the plans, after his attempt to negotiate failed, thereby giving the passionate hostility surrounding the venture some serious structure.

The flooding of the valley and village of Capel Celyn went ahead - the campaign highlighting a growing threat to the survival of Welsh-speaking communities and of the language itself.

S4C

The procrastination over establishing a Welsh language TV channel was done when S4C ('Sianel Pedwar Cymru') first broadcast programmes in 1982. Its inception had been proceeded by years of belligerence, the most extreme example being a threat by the Plaid Cymru leader of the time, Gwynfor Evans, to fast to death if Margaret Thatcher reneged on her commitment made in 1980 to set the channel up. The outcome, as a well-timed and well placed slogan at the House of Commons summed-up, was 'Gwynfor 1 - Thatcher 0'.

Previous to this the 'Pencarreg Three' had gained a huge amount of publicity for the cause by managing to switch off their local TV transmitter in 1979.

The Miners' Strike

Pit closures had been a constant black cloud for decades but the Miners' Strike of 1984, although not confined to Wales, became one of the most bitter industrial disputes of the 20th century. It has been well documented and successive generations still suffer because of it. One of the reassuring outcomes however, in a dearth of positives, is that the miners of Tower Colliery in south Wales used their redundancy cheques in a buy-out of the pit, creating a co-operative, effectively re-employing themselves.

Law

The Land of Song was once known as the Land of the White Gloves ('Gwlad y Menig Gwynion') on account of a tradition to hand a pair over to the judge in a court session if there had been no law breaking, and therefore, no cases to be heard.

Today, the Dyfed-Powys Police Authority covers more than half the land mass of the Principality (taking in Carmarthenshire, Ceredigion, Pembrokeshire and Powys) and is therefore the largest force in England and Wales. Its jurisdiction, some 160 miles, is greater than the distance between Cardiff and London.

Lawmakers

Hywel Dda

Created Wales' first formal legal system and documents drafted according to 'Cyfraith Hywel' (the (Law of Hywel Dda) survive to the present; as does his work on the legal status of women, the rights of illegitimate children and compensation for the victims of crime.

Largely building on the foundations laid by his grandfather, Rhodri Mawr, who created the kingdom of Deheubarth. The extensive geographical unit with its common legal system was, arguably, the closest there has ever been to a unified and independent Welsh state.

Dr William Price - Llantrisant

Dr William Price was a 19th century medic, herbalist, eccentric, druid and environmentalist who loved to wander the hills of his hometown naked.

While in his 80s he fathered a son - 'Iesu Grist' (Jesus Christ) - who unfortunately died in infancy. In January 1884 he burned the body near his home in a ritualistic ceremony he believed was in accordance with ancient Celtic practice (he had previously declared himself Archdruid of a lost Celtic faith). He was tried but not convicted, providing for the later legalisation of cremation.

Leo Abse - Cardiff

A Labour MP whose Private Members Bill made homosexuality legal in England and Wales.

Lawbreakers

Ruth Ellis - Rhyl

Became the last woman to be hanged in the UK after killing her lover outside a pub in Hampstead, north London, in 1955.

Outlaws and Pirates of Non-Penance

Twm Siôn Cati

16th century highwayman - Wales' own Robin Hood who pillaged around Carmarthenshire and

Cardiganshire. He would steal money and animals by disguising himself as a helpless beggar and hide the plunder in a cave at Llyn Brianne. Naturally - he later became a JP.

Bartu Ddu

Bartu Ddu or Black Bart (he had black hair) from Pembrokeshire was probably the most influential pirate ever. He became a notorious leader of a pirate company and up to 150 men that terrorised the Caribbean, virtually bringing trading there to a standstill, when the ship he was on off the west coast of African was captured. His doings made him fantastically rich - a fortune estimated in today's money of between £50 - £80 million.

The 'Jolly Roger' (skull and crossbones) pirates' flag is attributed to him. As he wore a red coat the French called him 'Le Joli Rouge', which became corrupted to Jolly Roger and eventually became synonymous with the flag.

Siôn Cwilt

The smuggler's patch around 1800 was Cardiganshire (commemorated in an area known today as Banc Siôn Cwilt) and Cwmtudu Cove in Newquay was his office.

Law Upholder

George ('The Hanging Judge') Jeffreys - *Wrexham*

George Jeffreys was the grandson of a judge in north Wales and decided on a career in law for himself, despite his parents' disapproval. Following his studies, he entered Gray's Inn and was later appointed Solicitor General to the Duke of York (later James II) and was knighted in 1677. He became recorder of London in 1678, Lord Chief Justice of England at 33 and then Lord Chancellor. In 1683 he was created Baron Jeffreys of Wem. He is known as 'Hanging Judge Jeffreys' because of the punishment he handed out at the trials of the supporters of the Duke of Monmouth.

Communication

Pioneers in Communication

William Henry Preece from Caernarvon brought the first telephones to UK - demonstrating them to Queen Victoria.

Treorchy born *Donald Davies* worked with the code breaker Alan Turing before developing 'Packet Switching'. It allows computers to communicate with each other and remains the basis of the internet.

Sir Terry (Celtic Manor Resort) Matthews' earlier business undertaking was a firm called Mitel which offered the first affordable push-button tone phones.

Reverse Telephone Directory

[Look up a 1471 area code before phoning your caller back - it might be your ageing aunt you've not spoken to for years or someone trying to contact you via a call centre before it moves to somewhere in Asia]

01239 Cardigan

01248 Bangor

01267 Carmarthen

01269 Ammanford

01286 Caernarvon

Communication

01291 Chepstow

01341 Barmouth

01348 Fishguard

01352 Mold

01407 Holyhead

01432 Hereford

01437 Haverfordwest Clynderwen

01443 Pontypridd

01446 Barry

01490 Corwen

01492 Colwyn Bay

01495 Pontypool

01497 Hay-on-Wye

01545 Llanarth

01547 Knighton

01550 Llandovery

01554 Llanelli

01558 Llandeilo

01559 Llandyssul

01566 Launceston

01570 Lampeter

01591 Llanwrtyd Wells

01597 Llandrindod Wells

01600 Monmouth

01633 Newport

01639 Neath

01643 Minehead

01646 Milford Haven

01650 Cemmacs Road

01654 Machynlleth

01656 Bridgend

01678 Bala

01685 Merthyr Tydfil

01686 Newtown Llanidloes

01690 Betws-y-Coed

01691 Oswestry

01743 Shrewsbury

01745 Rhyl

01758 Pwllheli

01766 Porthmadog

01792 Swansea

01824 Ruthin

01834 Narberth

01841 Newquay

01873 Abergavenny

01874 Brecon

01938 Welshpool

01946 Whitehaven

01970 Aberystwyth

01974 Llanon

01978 Wrexham

01982 Builth Wells

01993 Witney

01994 St Clears

029 Cardiff

Aviation

Bill Frost

Local legend puts inventor Bill Frost from Pembrokeshire in the air before the Wright brothers. His 'Flying Machine' apparently carried him above Saundersfoot in 1895...and into a tree.

Amy Johnson

Amy Johnson took off from Pendine sands in 1933 to begin the first successful east-west transatlantic flight.

UFOs

In the mid to late 1970s there were several reported sightings of UFOs in Pembrokeshire. Such was the paranormal activity that it gave rise to volumes of books and numerous articles documenting strange shaped aircraft and light formations. The geographical area became known as the 'Dyfed Triangle' and the official explanation was that these 'sightings' were actually of the frequent night flights from the nearby RAF base at Aberporth, while others considered that too much LSD had been left over from the 1960s.

Energy

The Centre for Alternative Technology, near Machynlleth, states that Wales is one of the world's leading developers of clean and sustainable energy.

A Guide to Renewable Energy Sites in Wales

Water Power

Over 100 years ago, engineers began to construct hydro power schemes on the upland streams of Wales.

Wind Power

The first large-scale wind farms appeared in the early 1990s. Since then, the turbines have become larger, more economical, efficient and quieter. In really windy locations, wind power is now competitive with other non-sustainable but more conventional methods of electricity generation. The UK now has some of the best wind resources in Europe.

Solar Power

Both electricity and heat can be provided by the sun. Photovoltaic (PV) modules are used to turn the sun's rays directly into electricity. There are several PV installations operating in Wales, the largest being a 12kWp array housed at the Centre for Alternative Technology. Solar power is also used to heat water for commercial or domestic purposes via solar collectors that are usually roof mounted. There are several examples of this technology on show around Wales, and it is said to work surprisingly well despite the country's weather.

Biomass

A well-established technology for the provision of heat and power in many European countries, such as Austria and Sweden, biomass is only beginning to catch on in Wales. The new National Botanical Garden of Wales has installed a biomass system which is providing heat for their greenhouse. Over the next ten years it seems likely that the use of biomass will grow substantially.

Brithdir Mawr Community

One of the growing communities utilising sustainable technologies is Brithdir Mawr Community in West Wales. Situated in Pembrokeshire it is an intentional collective of people governed by simplicity, sustainability and spirit within an Eco-village. They mentor several projects; taking care of the land, recycling and conserving resources, gardening and farming organically and are off the grid for electricity and water.

Resources

Athletics Association of Wales

BBC

Book of Useless Information - The Useless Information Society

Bwrdd yr Iaith Gymraeg (The Welsh Language Board)

Centre for Alternative Technology

Companies House

Countryside Council for Wales

Culturenet Cymru Ltd

DVLA

Dragon Soccer

Essential History of Rugby Union 1881-2003 by Steve Lewis and John Griffiths

Football Association of Wales

Glamorgan Cricket

Global Snooker Centre

Good Beer Guide

Guinness Book of Film Facts and Feats

HM Land Registry

Hansard

Hutchinson Factfinder (1998)

Idaho Welsh Society

National Welsh American Foundation

Office for National Statistics (2001 Census)

Oxford English Reference Dictionary

Portrait of the Artist as a Young Dog - introduction by Aeronwy Thomas

Rachel's Dairy

Tenovus

www.cawlcymru.co.uk

www.data-wales.co.uk

www.guildofglyndwr.co.uk

Wales and Cinema The First Hundred Years by David Berry

Wales Calling

Wales Tourist Board

Welsh Black Cattle Society

Welsh Pony and Cob Society

Welsh Rugby Union

Welsh Sheepdog Association

Wildlife Trusts

Index